# THE MINUTE TAKER'S HANDBOOK

# THE MINUTE TAKER'S HANDBOOK
## Taking minutes at any meeting with confidence

Jane Watson

**Self-Counsel Press**
(*a division of*)
International Self-Counsel Press Ltd.
Canada   U.S.A.

*Printed in Canada*

*First edition: March, 1992*
*Reprinted: February, 1993*


Canadian Cataloguing in Publication Data
Watson, Jane, 1948-
  The minute taker's handbook
  (Self-counsel reference series)
  Includes bibliographical references.
  ISBN 0-88908-994-9

 1. Meetings — Handbooks, manuals, etc.
2. Corporate minutes — Handbooks, manuals, etc.
I. Title.  II. Series.
HF5734.5.W38 1992  658.4'56  C92-091091-2


*Cover photography by Gary Ritchie Photography, Vancouver, B.C.*




**Self-Counsel Press**
*(a division of)*
International Self-Counsel Press Ltd.

| | |
|---|---|
| 1481 Charlotte Road | 1704 N. State Street |
| North Vancouver, B.C. | Bellingham, Washington |
| V7J 1H1 | 98225 |

*Dedicated with love to a supportive family and to the delegates of Humber College's Professional Symposium for Secretaries and Administrative Assistants who requested this book.*

# CONTENTS

# APPENDIXES

# SAMPLES

# PREFACE

A friend of mine related an incident about a series of meetings she attended many years ago shortly after she had graduated from university. The meetings were advertised in the local newspaper as an opportunity for the public to make their environmental concerns known to the government.

The number of people at the initial meeting was so large that the chair decided to break the audience down into smaller groups. Each group would then submit a separate proposal to him within the month.

My friend was slow off the mark in finding a group to join and so was placed in a group of 12 businessmen. Her arrival was greeted with a relieved look on the faces of some members. One unthinking male seemed to reflect the feelings of the entire group when he said, "Oh wonderful, a woman! Now we have someone to take the minutes."

My friend was upset. She felt that she had a contribution to make but now she was being relegated to the back seat. Anyway, she did become the recording secretary, albeit ungraciously. Moreover, all of her ideas were patronized or ignored!

I can say only that my friend was inexperienced and didn't understand the important role of the minutes or the minute taker in a meeting.

While I don't agree with the view expressed by one meeting expert that the person "with power without limits is the one who takes the minutes," I do believe that the minute taker has a vital role within the meeting structure and can choose to use his or her responsibilities wisely or not.

For a short time, my friend had legitimate, easy access to several important business people that other people would have loved to have had. She could easily have phoned them to check on remarks made in their meetings, but she didn't. She viewed the whole process as a boring task to be completed as quickly as possible. As she was also job hunting at the time, I am surprised by her lack of foresight.

Knowing my friend, I also assume that her comments at the meetings were overlooked not because she was the minute taker, but because of poor body language and a lack of presentation skills.

Nowadays, meetings play a major role in both business and volunteer organizations, and one of the key people required to make the meetings effective is the minute taker.

No matter who you are, being the minute taker can —

(a) give you easy access to other members in the group,

(b) keep you up to date on what is going on within the organization,

(c) enable you to help the chair accomplish the goals of the meeting, and

(d) keep you more focused on what is being said so that your comments are relevant and your interpretation of what happened is accurate.

However, there are men and women still behaving either like my friend or like the unenlightened man in the meeting years ago: people who don't realize the importance of minute taking and how to use it to their advantage; people who make any excuse to avoid being appointed recording secretary; and people who are intimidated by the thought of having to take minutes, unsure of what to put in, and fearful of missing important details.

This book is for them. It is designed to help all people who are involved in the minute-taking process, either on an occasional or regular basis, become more confident in their recording skills. In addition, it provides techniques and examples to enable minute takers to produce concise, accurate minutes in a timely manner for both formal and informal meetings.

# 1

## ANYONE FOR A MEETING?

No matter who you are or what you do, whether at work or in the community, you are involved in meetings.

They may be of an impromptu nature — in the hallway or the cafeteria — or they may be long, formal meetings held in council chambers at regular intervals. However, there is no escape; today everyone is involved in meetings of some sort or other.

Statistics show that in North America the average manager or technical professional now spends nearly one-quarter of his or her total work week in meetings while upper and middle managers spend nearly two days a week. Moreover, experts predict that the frequency of meetings will increase, not decrease.

These statistics contradict the widely held belief that new technologies will reduce the need for face-to-face encounters. This view has been supported particularly by many sales organizations that believe the less you see of a salesperson at the office, the more likely it is that the employee is out making sales. Companies and individuals who accepted this idea purchased "timesaving" devices to cut down on the need for meetings. Some sales representatives turned their cars into mobile offices with car phones, fax machines, lap-top computers, electronic organizers, and post-it notes on dashboards.

However, managers are now finding that it is important to see their salespeople regularly to ensure that everyone is staying on target. One sales representative for a large computer company spent weeks trying to convince a new customer to buy a software package that the company no longer marketed — regular sales and marketing meetings would have prevented this from happening.

Professor John Kotter of the Harvard Business School, who has conducted studies on the managerial workload, has found that managers tend to accomplish their objectives better by talking directly to people. "Car phones and fax machines have little positive effect on relationship building [which] tends to be done face to face," says Kotter.

Besides building relationships, meetings provide an opportunity to —

- deliver information to a group of people,
- ensure that everyone receives the same information at the same time,
- reduce tensions and conflicts by bringing them out in the open,
- initiate problem solving or decision sharing,
- keep misunderstandings to a minimum,
- plan an event,
- arrange work assignments,
- nominate officers,
- investigate an issue,
- plot strategies,
- plan budgets, and
- prepare reports.

Granted, many meetings are impromptu and often decisions are made by the elevator or on the way out to lunch. One manager claims his most productive meetings take place in the parking lot — but most meetings are of a prescribed, highly formal nature and are run by a chair.

## a. TYPES OF MEETINGS

Formal meetings can be divided into two types: organizational and operational.

### 1. Organizational meetings

There are two types of organizational meetings: annual general meetings for shareholders or members of an organization, and regular meetings of representative bodies, such as boards of directors and management committee meetings.

#### (a) Annual general meetings

The charters or bylaws of many large companies and non-profit organizations require that an annual general meeting be held at which shareholders or members may vote on policy changes and proposed large projects.

At a corporate annual general meeting, the chief executive officer (CEO) generally makes a speech highlighting the company's activities over the past year and announcing plans for the future. This type of meeting ranges from a modest function to a large, glitzy media event.

For non-profit organizations or co-ops, the annual general meeting provides members with the opportunity to review the financial affairs of the organization and, perhaps, elect a new board of directors for the upcoming year.

#### (b) Board meetings

A board meeting is attended by representatives appointed or elected to coordinate the work of the organization. Boards differ in the degree to which they are involved with the day-to-day issues of an organization. However, they meet at regular intervals and are bound by law to produce minutes.

### 2. Operational meetings

The following are examples of operational meetings:

(a)  Corporate planning

(b) Committee

(c) Staff

(d) Sales

For all of these types of meetings, it is essential that accurate minutes be taken and distributed.

### (a) Corporate planning meetings

Corporate planning meetings are organized to direct the operations of a company. They can vary in length from one day to one week and can be held on or off site. The best corporate planning meetings are usually those that combine formal planning sessions with time to interact informally with colleagues.

### (b) Committee meetings

Committees are appointed to carry out specific tasks under the jurisdiction of a larger body. Because of their smaller size, they are usually better able to work on policy or administrative details. Committees and their meetings are the mainstay of non-profit organizations that might employ volunteers on, for example, a fund-raising committee, special events committee, or newsletter committee.

Committees are usually designated as either *standing* or *ad hoc*. A standing committee is permanently established to deal with a regular issue, department, or activity, such as administration or operations. Members of standing committees are appointed or elected for a clearly established term.

An ad hoc committee is created for a special function, and when the function is completed the committee is dissolved. A company might form an ad hoc "building committee," for example, to investigate the feasibility of purchasing real estate for a new head office. A non-profit organization might form an ad hoc committee to organize a special twenty-fifth anniversary event.

4

### (c) Staff meetings

Staff meetings are normally chaired by a manager and held on a regular basis. They are used as a vehicle to convey information to and from upper management in a company.

### (d) Sales meetings

Sales meetings are held to motivate the participants to sell more products or services or to provide new product information.

## b. THE ESSENTIAL ELEMENTS OF A MEETING

It doesn't matter why, when, or where you hold a meeting, it is costly. Even if it is held in a company boardroom, there are still salaries and time factors to consider. A staff of 12 that meets 2 hours a week for 50 weeks a year involves 1,200 hours of time. If each of the 12 are professionals earning approximately $50 an hour, the yearly cost to hold these meetings would be $60,000. And this doesn't take into account the time spent preparing for or traveling to the meeting. If you also add company overhead, the costs double.

Costs are even more important for the non-profit organization, in which every dollar spent must be carefully accounted for to its members. As well, most non-profit groups have very tight budgets. For both businesses and less formal groups, it is important for meetings to be conducted in a time-efficient and cost-effective manner.

To ensure that meetings are productive and worth the expense involved, two ingredients are necessary:

(a) A strong chair

(b) Accurate minutes

Most people feel that many of the meetings they attend are a waste of time and an exercise in boredom. In a survey by Accountemps, a personnel agency, 200 executives of the 1,000 largest corporations in the United States were asked by an independent market research firm about the amount of time they spend in unnecessary meetings. It was found that the average American business executive feels that he or she spends 72 minutes a day — or 288 hours a year — in unnecessary meetings.

## 1. A strong chair

The word "strong" does not refer to physical strength or the ability to roar over participants. Strength, in this case, refers to the ability of the chair to help the group achieve its goals within a specific time frame.

It also involves the strength to permit all sides of an argument to be heard and the expertise to keep the meeting and its members on track. A strong chair acts as a traffic cop directing the flow of the discussion and issuing stop and go instructions. In addition, the chair should have the wisdom to cancel the meeting if its purpose can be achieved in another manner, such as a one-on-one discussion.

## 2. Accurate minutes

Someone once said that if the minutes of a meeting are not accurate then the meeting might just as well not have taken place. This is true.

People don't always remember exactly what happened in a meeting, or they may have understood the details a little differently than the speaker intended. They may have taken copious notes, but either don't refer to them later or can't interpret what they wrote. They may look as though they are listening attentively, but afterward you find that their minds were on other matters.

In one study, researchers taped a meeting of the Cambridge Psychological Society. Two weeks later, the meeting participants were interviewed to find out how much they really remembered of what had occurred. The average participant remembered only 8% of what had happened at the meeting and of this 8%, 42% was incorrect to some degree. A couple of people even remembered things that hadn't happened at all.

If people can't remember or agree on what actually occurred at a meeting, how can the group efficiently accomplish its objectives?

The answer, of course, is through the minutes. Minutes should be written to provide all the members with the following information:

(a) How the issues were discussed and finally resolved

(b) The names of those individuals who were assigned specific tasks and the dates they are to be completed.

There are several types of minutes. If a meeting is run informally, detailed minutes and a person to produce them are not necessary. The group leader can simply write a memo or "action minutes" after the meeting. On the other hand, a meeting conducted according to parliamentary procedure should be followed up by formal minutes, and someone should be designated as the official minute taker.

The most common complaints of minute takers are the following:

- Weak chair, unable to keep the participants on track

- Speakers who mumble, ramble, or speak too fast

- Speakers who are disorganized

- Chairs and speakers who give vague directions

- Speakers who ask the minute taker to create a motion around their comments

- Too many people talking at once

- Distractions — phones ringing, people making irrelevant comments

- Not following the agenda

- An impossible number of items on the agenda

- Motions being made at top speed
- Speakers not identifying themselves/the chair not identifying speakers
- Negative people
- Power-hungry people
- Unprepared members
- Not being allowed to have a break when the members have one
- Being sent out of the meeting to make coffee, phone calls, or photocopies

This book provides information on the role of the minute taker and the chair and on the preparation of formal, semi-formal, and action minutes. By using this book and preparing for meetings at which you have to act as minute taker, you can eliminate most, if not all, of the problems presented in the list above.

In addition, I have included guidelines on other areas with which the minute taker should be familiar: parliamentary procedure, the importance of the agenda, the use of electronic devices, and the hidden variables that affect the process of taking minutes.

# 2
# MEETINGS AND THEIR PARTICIPANTS

In a play, the actors must understand both their roles and the purpose of the production in order for the play to reach a successful outcome.

Meetings operate in the same fashion. The participants are more likely to accomplish their objectives efficiently if they understand the objectives of the meeting and know the role they are to play — whether it be the part of chair, minute taker, or participant.

## a. MEETING OBJECTIVES

Different meetings have different objectives. A good agenda plays an important role in outlining a meeting's objectives and should be prepared for every meeting. (Agendas are discussed in detail in chapter 10.)

It is essential for the chair of the meeting to have a clear understanding of the goals so that he or she can conduct the meeting in an organized fashion and guide the participants to a successful achievement of their purpose.

Minute takers who know the objectives of the meeting will also find their job easier as they will understand what is essential to include in the minutes. For example, if the objective of a meeting is to divide the workload of a particular project among the participants, then every task, the name of the person carrying it out, and the deadline must appear in the minutes. Unnecessary comments, such as who carried out similar tasks in the past and the personal feelings of the members regarding the project, would be omitted.

It is also useful for each participant to understand the meeting's objectives so that he or she will come to the meeting prepared to contribute. Sometimes a participant may feel that the group's purpose has little relevance to his or her area of expertise and may suggest that another person's attendance would be more effective, thereby saving a company or organization time and money.

Meeting objectives fall into four categories, depending on the nature of the topic being discussed:

- To solve a problem
- To reach a decision
- To provide information
- To develop a creative idea

## 1. Problem solving

When a situation arises that a person or the group is uncomfortable or unhappy with, a meeting may be called to resolve the problem. The meeting leader must first ensure that all the participants recognize that a problem exists and that they wish to make the effort to solve it.

## 2. Decision making

A meeting with the objective of making a decision is different from a problem-solving meeting because the decision formulated usually involves some degree of risk to the members. The chair must be certain that the group has the power to make the decision. In small meetings, decisions are usually arrived at by consensus. In larger meetings, a formal vote may be taken.

## 3. Information sharing

A meeting to share information is often abused. Many managers call regular staff meetings to share information, but the hidden agenda is really to determine whether everyone is doing his or her job. These meetings can become boring as people take turns reporting on their activities.

A meeting leader should determine whether the meeting is essential or if the information would be better presented in written format or dealt with on a one-on-one basis.

### 4. Creativity

Any organization may hold creative meetings from time to time: a non-profit group might hold a brainstorming session to develop new fund-raising ideas; a housing cooperative might reformulate certain policies; the marketing department of a business might meet to design the launch of a new product. Participants at creative meetings discuss, modify, and refine ideas through interaction with the other participants.

The meeting leader must walk a fine line to ensure that the participants are kept on target but are not so rigidly controlled that creative juices are stifled. It is important that everyone's ideas be given equal hearing.

### 5. Overlapping objectives

On occasion, an information-sharing meeting can turn into a problem-solving one if a troublesome issue is raised. The meeting leader must decide if the participants have the time and background knowledge to deal adequately with the subject or whether it should be referred to a future meeting.

The leader should also know whether the group has the authority to reach a decision on the problem or whether the information should be passed on to another authority.

Nevertheless, it is important that the leader understand the stages that the group may travel through and ensure that it does not spend excess time on situations that its members are not prepared or authorized to handle.

I recall one meeting that was initially intended as an information exchange. But someone suggested a new advertising campaign for a section of the organization, and after three hours of creative discussion, a draft proposal was formulated. Later, it was found that the head of the section concerned was vehemently opposed to any such campaign. If the chair had postponed the discussion until she had talked to the manager, three hours of company time may have been put to more productive use.

## b. THE MEETING PERSONNEL

The personnel at a meeting or the roles to be filled are the leader, the minute taker, and the participants. Whenever a group of people get together, it is interesting to watch them slip into their appointed roles with little conscious effort.

### 1. The meeting leader

Someone always seems to surface to assume the role of leader: someone who is prepared to issue commands and get things moving. Ideally, the person who assumes the role of leader is also the person officially appointed to act in that capacity. Difficulties can arise in meetings when the official leader does not wish to assume the role or does not understand what the role entails. Power struggles between would-be and official leaders also create dissension within the group. When this happens, taking minutes and achieving the goals of the meeting become difficult if not impossible.

The leader must understand his or her responsibilities and carry them out. The meeting leader can operate under a variety of titles: chair, chairman, chairwoman, chairperson, president, moderator, or presiding officer. But regardless of the title, the role is the same. In this book, I refer to the meeting leader as the chair.

Incidentally, many parliamentarians feel that "chairwoman" or "chairperson" are extremely awkward words and believe that in meetings the presiding officer should be addressed as "Mr. Chairman" or "Madam Chairman" regardless of whether the presiding officer is a man or woman. However, if the organization has nothing in its rules stating how the chair is to be addressed, the best guideline to follow is to let the chair be called whatever he or she feels is appropriate. The chair must inform the meeting of his or her preference as soon as possible.

The competent chair —

(a) understands the objectives of the meeting,

(b) ensures that the agenda is prepared and circulated beforehand,

(c) ensures that necessary material and staff resources are available,

(d) is knowledgeable about parliamentary procedures, especially if the meeting is conducted on a formal basis,

(e) starts the meeting on time,

(f) introduces and welcome all newcomers,

(g) makes a clear statement of the issues to be discussed,

(h) sees that basic facts are stated accurately and fully,

(i) assigns the floor to whomever wishes to speak,

(j) restricts discussion of opinions or experiences whenever facts are available,

(k) ensures that each side of an issue is fully and fairly stated,

(l) restricts emotional and tactless remarks,

(m) sees that no one dominates the discussion,

(n) makes frequent verbal summaries of the conclusions reached,

(o) restates all motions, amendments, and the outcome of the voting,

(p) names the proposers and seconders of motions if these names are to appear in the minutes,

(q) casts the deciding vote in the case of a tie,

(r) sets the time and date for a future meeting,

(s) ends the meeting on time, and

(t)  ensures that there is some type of meeting follow-up, either by memo or by action or formal minutes.

The bylaws of the organization may also assign other duties to the chair.

For a complete discussion of the role of the chair and how to effectively run a meeting, see *Chairing a Meeting With Confidence*, another title in the Self-Counsel Series.

## 2. The minute taker

The minute taker may also act under many names: recording secretary, secretary, note taker, recorder. In a small informal meeting, the chair may act as recorder, but this is not recommended for most meetings as it prevents the chair from devoting his or her full attention to the discussion.

According to *Robert's Rules of Order*, if the chair is absent and there is no deputy present, the secretary should call the meeting to order and preside over it until the group elects a chair *pro tem* (for the time being).

As minute taker, your other duties will vary according to your position within the meeting framework. If you are an officer of the organization, you will not have the "housekeeping" tasks normally assigned to a minute taker who is also the office secretary. (These tasks are discussed in chapters 5 and 11.)

No matter what your position within the organization, however, as minute taker you must be able to handle the following duties:

(a)  Sort out the comments, suggested actions, and decisions expressed at the meeting and produce an accurate summation within a reasonable time period.

(b)  Keep track of the attendance at meetings.

(c)  Store the minutes of the organization and all related materials, except those particularly assigned to others.

(d) Find previous mention of an issue in earlier minutes if requested.

(e) Provide the chair of each committee with a list of the members of his or her committee and the papers and instructions pertaining to it.

(f) Inform the chair of the activities that have been referred to the upcoming meeting.

(g) Read aloud all correspondence sent to the assembly.

(h) Request that the chair temporarily halt the meeting if comments are flowing so fast that it is impossible to make an accurate summation.

(i) Authenticate all the records and documents associated with the meeting by having the chair add his or her signature.

(j) Bring a copy of the constitution, bylaws, and the standing rules of the organization to every meeting.

(k) Be familiar with the parliamentary procedures used by the assembly.

(l) Carry on all official correspondence for the organization. (When this duty involves a great deal of work, it is frequently assigned to a correspondence secretary.)

To function properly as a minute taker, you must be alert, highly organized, and focused on the group discussion in order to restate the positions of others accurately and objectively. Not everyone is capable of being a good minute taker.

I once heard a workshop leader say "I now want you to divide into smaller groups to discuss … I know it is early in the morning, so anyone who is feeling a little tired or hasn't quite woken up yet can be the recorder." Wrong, wrong, wrong!

A minute taker must be —

(a) a good listener,

(b) a sound critical thinker, and

(c)  an excellent organizer.

In some organizations where the chair changes every year but the minute taker is appointed for an indefinite period, the secretary is the officer of most importance within the group. This is because he or she is familiar with the history of the group and the motions that have been made, and can explain to the chair how things have been done in the past and how they should be done in the future.

If you are the minute taker at a formal hearing, you will not have a voice in the proceedings unless you are also an official member of the organization. In less formal meetings, you may be expected to contribute your ideas and opinions, and then you must be able to operate on two wave lengths: as a typical participant, who listens and interacts, and also as the one who processes the information.

The habits of a good recorder are similar to those of a good chair. Good minute takers often become equally competent chairs. At informal meetings, the minute taker's role can be regularly reassigned among the members, which can be one of the best methods for developing future leaders in meeting management.

Although the ability to take shorthand is an asset, notes can just as easily be taken in longhand or typed directly onto a computer. Except for motions, minutes are not recorded verbatim but are merely a summation of what has occurred.

### 3.  The participants

Meeting participants also have their roles to play, and they are as responsible as the chair and the minute taker for achieving a meeting's objectives. Meetings are also a good place for participants to showcase their capabilities.

Meeting participants should —

(a)  arrive on time,

(b) be prepared by reading reports or agendas beforehand and bringing them to the meeting,

(c) read the minutes of the past meeting to ensure that they are accurate and that all assigned activities have been carried out,

(d) focus on the meeting,

(e) listen carefully to all ideas,

(f) ask questions if a statement is unclear,

(g) participate fully in discussions but not dominate them or allow others to do so,

(h) look for the positive portion of another's ideas,

(i) avoid petty arguments and wisecracks,

(j) avoid being defensive if ideas are criticized,

(k) have all handouts photocopied before the meeting,

(l) warn the chair in advance if bringing up a controversial topic,

(m) inform the chair in advance if leaving early,

(n) pass a note of explanation to the chair if called away unexpectedly, then leave quickly, and

(o) shake hands firmly when the meeting is breaking up.

If the meeting is a formal one, the participant has some additional responsibilities, such as —

(p) put complicated motions in writing,

(q) address all questions through the chair, and

(r) be familiar with parliamentary procedure.

## c. MEETING AGREEMENT

In order for a meeting to be effective, in other words, for the meeting to accomplish its goals in a timely fashion, everyone must work together as a team. Each member of the team must fulfill his or her own role and assist — or at least, not hinder — the other members in carrying out their duties.

However, sometimes group members — and it may be the chair, the minute taker, or a participant — do not carry out their responsibilities, either because they don't want to or because they don't fully understand what is expected. Or perhaps one member may prevent others from completing their tasks efficiently.

A common complaint among meeting participants is, I could do a much better job but ..., and participants go on to complain about another member of the group: the chair is weak or disorganized, the recording secretary can't take accurate minutes, or another member constantly tries to dominate discussions.

Yet participants may feel uncomfortable discussing the issue especially if the "problem" member holds a higher position in the office hierarchy, is a long-standing member of the group, or is serving in a volunteer capacity.

With this in mind and with the help of a number of people who have spent a great deal of time in meetings, I have devised three meeting agreement forms to be signed by all members of a group (see Samples #1, #2, and #3). The forms are similar to a contract in that each player or member reads what is expected of him or her and by signing it agrees to carry out certain tasks.

Please note that the agreements are designed to serve as a starting point. The forms can be easily customized to meet the specific needs of your organization.

The form could be given to a new member of the meeting team before the first assembly or used as a starting point for a more detailed conversation with someone who does not seem aware of his or her responsibilities within the group.

**The Chair:**

To ensure that the ABC Committee conducts its business in an efficient manner, I *(person's name)*, the chair of the committee, hereby promise to do the following:

1. Give all the meeting participants adequate warning of an upcoming meeting.

2. Prepare a detailed agenda.

3. Allow all sides of an argument to be heard.

4. Encourage all members to participate in a discussion.

5. Restate all motions before a vote is taken and then state the outcome.

6. Insist that complicated motions and resolutions be submitted in writing.

7. Avoid sending the minute taker out of the room during the meeting to run errands.

8. Permit the minute taker to take a break when the group does.

9. Be familiar with the parliamentary procedures used to govern the assembly.

_____

**Chair**

**The Recording Secretary:**

To ensure that the ABC Committee conducts its business in an efficient manner, I *(person's name)*, the recording secretary of the committee, hereby promise to do the following:

1. Notify the chair of any unfinished business, motions, or reports that are due at the upcoming meeting.

2. Send out all agendas and accompanying material promptly.

3. Make arrangements for any necessary equipment or refreshments.

4. Arrive at the meeting at least 15 minutes early.

5. Be prepared and organized and have any required photocopying completed.

6. Alert the chair when a quorum is present.

7. Provide the organization with objective, accurate minutes.

8. Be familiar with the parliamentary procedures used to govern the assembly.

_____

**Recording Secretary**

**The Meeting Participant:**

To ensure that the ABC Committee conducts its business in an efficient manner, I *(person's name)*, hereby promise to do the following:

1. Read the agenda and all accompanying material, including the previous minutes, before the meeting.

2. Bring all necessary reports and information to the meeting.

3. Be prepared to discuss the items on the agenda.

4. Avoid emotional and tactless remarks.

5. Address all remarks through the chair.

6. Put all complicated motions and resolutions in writing.

7. Listen to the remarks of others with an open mind.

8. Give everyone an equal chance to speak.

9. Avoid asking the recording secretary to run errands for me during the meeting.

10. Be familiar with the parliamentary procedures used to govern the assembly.

_____

**Meeting Participant**

# 3

## MINUTES FOR FORMAL MEETINGS

### a. GOOD MINUTES PROVIDE A RECORD OF THE MEETING

Minutes are a permanent, formal record of what went on in a meeting. Their purpose is to provide the members of a group with —

- a clear, objective summary of the group's activities,

- a means of conveying information to people who were unable to attend the meeting,

- a reminder of future expected action, and

- an historical background of the decisions of the group and the rationale behind them.

When approved, minutes of meetings are considered official documents and can be used as evidence in legal proceedings. Minutes may be written in a variety of styles: formal, semiformal, or action. The choice of style is based on the nature of the meeting and on the dictates of the bylaws and/or the committee itself.

Formal minutes support a meeting which is governed by a chair according to a parliamentary code (see chapter 6). Semiformal or action minutes are used by small groups which do not have a clearly defined operating structure.

The rest of this chapter is devoted to formal minutes. Chapter 4 deals with organizing the minutes for informal meetings.

## b. PROPERLY RECORDED MINUTES

Some people make the mistake of thinking that minutes must be verbatim to be proper. However, this is rarely the case and is usually not practical. Most organizations, with the exception of judicial bodies, do not need a detailed record of all the comments at a meeting. Word-for-word documents are too time-consuming to prepare and to read. Moreover, few minute takers can take shorthand at approximately 250 words per minute — the speed required for verbatim minute taking.*

With the exception of the motions, which should be recorded word for word, there is some latitude in the amount of detail included in the minutes. Some groups want the minutes to be a comprehensive outline of everything that was discussed so that the organization's activities and decisions can be easily justified. Other groups feel that background information is not essential and that only the members need to understand the remarks.

Years ago, a committee that was concerned with public hearings relating to changes in municipal bylaws had very comprehensive minutes. Every decision was preceded by a detailed rationale. With the appointment of a new chair, this was changed. Now, the minutes read "passed in accordance with Section 345 of the Zoning Bylaw."

Both styles are correct. It is, therefore, important that you, as minute taker, know precisely what type of minutes the committee expects to receive and can deliver them consistently.

More discussion about the details that are usually included in minutes is found in chapter 5.

---

*If your organization requires verbatim documentation and you do not have anyone on staff with the skill or time to undertake the task, hire a freelance court reporter or tape the meeting and have it transcribed later by an outside organization. Agencies, such as Farr and Associates Reporting Inc. of Toronto and Associated Reporters of New York, provide transcription services anywhere in the world through electronic recording devices and telecommunications.

## c. ORGANIZING FORMAL MINUTES

Formal minutes follow the same organizational pattern as a formal meeting:

1. Heading
2. Attendance
3. Minutes of previous meetings
4. Reports
5. Finances
6. Correspondence
7. Unfinished business (or business arising from previous meeting)
8. New business
9. Adjournment
10. Next meeting: date and time
11. Signatures

In formal meetings, decisions are reached through motions. Motions are proposals placed before the members for debate and voting. You must record these verbatim in the appropriate section of the minutes. Examples of how motions are recorded appear later in this chapter.

The samples in this section show how to lay out various portions of formal minutes (see Samples #4, #5, and #6). A complete set of sample formal minutes is shown in Sample #7.

### 1. Heading

The heading should be 1 inch (2.5 cm) from the top of the page. Each heading line should be centered and be typed in either capitals or in upper- and lowercase letters depending on the organization's official style. The heading should include the word "Minutes" and also the name of the committee or group holding the meeting. There is no firm rule about

### FUND-RAISING COMMITTEE
### CREDIT VALLEY HOSPITAL
### REGULAR MONTHLY MEETING
### MINUTES

December 2, 199-                7:00 p.m.
Main Floor Boardroom

**Present:**

Michael Cockburn (Chair)
Angela Andreachi
Sabrina Anzini
Alisa Chiovetti
Marcus Sconci
Jeff Chin (Recording Secretary)

**Absent:**

John Watson
Bill Jones

**In attendance:**

Michael Amesbury

## MINUTES
## FUND-RAISING COMMITTEE
## CREDIT VALLEY HOSPITAL

A special meeting of the Credit Valley Fund-raising Committee was held on April 15 at 7:30 p.m. at South Hall Community Center. Mr. Michael Cockburn, Chair, presided.

**Present:** Angela Andreachi (Secretary), Ryan Mitchell, Marcus Sconci, Sarah Thiffault, Greg Valliquette, Timothy Watson, Marlene Zuliani.

**Unable to be present:** Rosemary Rock, Betty Steinhauer

**In attendance:** Brian Madigan

A regular monthly meeting of the Credit Valley Hospital was held on the 15th day of April, at 7:30 p.m. in the hospital's main floor boardroom, with Mr. Michael Cockburn presiding. The secretary being absent, Ms. Julia Richards was appointed secretary pro tem. The minutes were read and approved.

*or*

## MINUTES OF THE PREVIOUS MEETING OF JULY 10, 199-

MOTION: It was MOVED, SECONDED, and CARRIED

"That the minutes of the meeting of July 10, 199- be approved as printed."

*or*

## MINUTES OF THE PREVIOUS MEETING

The minutes of the July 10, 199-, meeting were approved as read.

## MINUTES
## COUNCIL OF THE TOWN OF RED OAKS

A regular monthly meeting of the Council of the Town of Red Oaks was held on May 20, 199- at 7:00 p.m. in the Council Chambers.

**Present:** Mayor Albert Brooks (Chair), Regional Councillors, Suzanne Watson (Recording Secretary), and Laura Cockburn, and Councillors, Adam Kodeda, Mary Saito, Bruce Green, Michael Miller, and Ryan Duchak.

**Absent:** Councillor Robert Seymour

**Staff members in attendance:** Jennifer Becevello, Clerk; W.J. Kelley, Commissioner of Planning; Joan Bowen, C.E.O. Library Board; and Peter Jansen, Secretary.

### Previous Minutes

Minutes of the April 16, 199- meeting were approved as circulated.

### Reports

1. Red Oaks Public Library Board
Motion: It was moved by Regional Councillor Watson and seconded by Councillor Kodeda that the report of the Library Board be received. Motion passed.

*aB*

2. Red Oaks Arena Association
Motion: It was moved by Councillor Miller and seconded by Councillor Duchak that the report of the Arena Association be received.
Motion passed.

**Unfinished Business**

Waste Management and Reduction Calendar

Motion: It was moved by Councillor Duchak and seconded by Councillor Saito:

"That Council approve the draft Waste Management and Reduction calendar as presented at this meeting;

That the contract for printing be awarded to Towne Crier Inc.; and,

That certain details be added to the historical section of the calendar."

Amending Motion: It was moved by Councillor Watson and seconded by Councillor Miller that the motion be amended to include the words "for a fee not to exceed $19,260.00." The amending motion and the main motion carried.

**New Business**

Reduction of Speed Limit — Avery Avenue
Staff Report SRW.9X.76

Bylaw 434-9X — A Bylaw to Restrict the Speed of Motor Vehicles on Avery Avenue (To reduce the speed limit on Avery Avenue to 40 miles per hour).

*AB*

Motion: It was moved by Councillor Duchak and seconded by Councillor Saito that Bylaw 434-9X be given first reading. Motion carried.

Request to Remove Fence Requirements — Miller Boulevard

Mr. P. Thomas, representing the residents of Miller Boulevard, requested that the fencing requirements for properties on McCallum Drive backing onto the valley land be removed.

Motion: It was moved by Regional Councillor Cockburn and seconded by Councillor Miller that Council postpone consideration of this request until the Parks, Recreation, and Culture Committee can report on all aspects of the fencing. Motion carried.

Peter Jansen is to notify the Chair of the Parks, Recreation, and Culture Committee that a representative of that committee must be present at Council's next meeting to discuss the fencing issue.

The Chair adjourned the meeting at 9:45 p.m.

The next meeting will be held in the Council Chambers at 7:00 p.m. on June 19, 199-.

*S. Watson*
_____
Secretary

*Albert Brooks*
_____
Chair

which line should come first, but be consistent. Use the same style for all of an organization's minutes and agendas.

The place, time, and date of the meeting may be placed in the heading or in an introductory paragraph as shown in Samples #4 and #5. If the meeting location always remains the same, it may be omitted.

In formal style, the minutes should state whether the meeting is a special or a regular one (e.g., weekly, monthly, or yearly).

### 2. Attendance

You must include the names of both the people who attended the meeting and those who were invited but did not attend. You can list these casually, in alphabetical order, or according to office hierarchy. Sometimes the attendance record is necessary to show a quorum, so for this reason you must record the time of a member's late arrival or early departure. List people who are not regular members as "in attendance."

You should also record who chaired the meeting and your name as the recording secretary.

### 3. Minutes of previous meetings

At the beginning of a meeting, the chair asks the members to approve or amend the minutes of the last meeting. The decision regarding the minutes may be placed in the introductory paragraph or listed separately as shown in Sample #6.

Although you can record this decision as an official motion, it is preferable to use the following standard forms depending on the situation:

(a) When the minutes were distributed, read, and approved at the meeting —

*Minutes of the June 10, 199-, meeting were approved as read.*

(b) When the minutes were distributed earlier but approved at the meeting —

*Minutes of the June 10, 199-, meeting were approved as printed/circulated.*

(c) When a member or members do not agree with some of the wording in the minutes for the last meeting and agree to a change —

*Minutes of the June 10, 199-, meeting were approved with corrections.*

(Please refer to chapter 5 for more information on how to handle corrections in previous minutes.)

(d) When the minutes were not read —

*The reading of the minutes was dispensed with.*

-or-

*The reading of the minutes was deferred until ….*

## 4. Reports

This section refers to the reports received from any of the group's officers, such as the treasurer, and from any standing or ad hoc (special) committees connected with the group.

As minute taker, you must summarize any reports or other documents presented at the meeting and then either attach them to the minutes as an appendix or refer to them in the minutes as filed.

If the report was sent to the group for information purposes only, indicate that the report "was received."

If someone conveyed the information orally, or accompanied the report with a verbal explanation, indicate that the report was "presented."

If the report contains a statement of opinion and facts and concludes with resolutions, then you should record that the report was "adopted" or "accepted." A report could also be "considered" if the group wants to look at it further and vote on its "adoption" at a later date.

When the assembly decides to "adopt" a committee's resolutions, enter the resolutions in full into the minutes. With a particularly important report, the assembly may order it "to be entered in the minutes." In that case, you must include the complete report in the minutes.

After someone moves either to "accept" or to "adopt" a report, the report is then open to amendment by the assembly.

### 5. Finances

Finances are usually discussed under the treasurer's report, which is often just a report on the amount of money on hand, or it may be a more detailed listing of income and expenditures since the previous meeting, cash on hand, obligations outstanding, and a balance. No action is required on this type of report.

In fact, it is technically improper to move that the treasurer's report be approved unless it has been audited because until it is, no one can be assured that it is accurate. The presiding officer should simply thank the officer or, if it is a written report, indicate that it will be filed.

A treasurer's annual report is different. It will be in a written form and should be audited according to instructions in the bylaws. Then a motion and a vote is required on accepting the auditor's report.

### 6. Correspondence

Letters sent to the group are usually read by the secretary and then either filed or attached to the appendix of the minutes. Telegrams, fax messages, and telephone conversations may also be discussed in this section.

### 7. Unfinished business (business arising from previous meeting)

This section involves motions or issues raised at earlier meetings and deferred to the current meeting, details of follow-up actions, and new actions as a result of previously handled business.

## 8. New business

This portion of the meeting and the minutes is devoted to the introduction of new information. It may also include the assigning of specific tasks to members of the group and the setting of deadlines.

## 9. Adjournment

To adjourn the meeting, the chair may call for a motion to adjourn, in which case it would appear in the minutes as a motion, or he or she might close the meeting after ensuring that there is no further business to be discussed. As minute taker, you would then record:

> *The chair adjourned the meeting at 11:30 a.m.*

> -or-

> *There being no further business, the meeting was adjourned at 11:30 a.m.*

## 10. Next meeting

Record the date, time, and location of the next meeting.

## 11. Signatures

The closing phrase "Respectfully submitted" is usually omitted nowadays, as it is considered old-fashioned. However, some highly formal groups still insist on it.

The minute taker's signature and title appear at the end of the minutes. Some minute takers also include the date when the typing of the final minutes was completed so the time lapse between the meeting and the actual coverage is evident. This step is optional.

In formal minutes, the chair initials all pages of the minutes and signs the last page to prevent any alterations.

## d. MOTIONS

### 1. Recording motions in the minutes

In formal style, all properly made motions must be included in the minutes. Generally, to be proper, a motion must be moved and seconded. The exception is a motion made in a committee meeting; committee meetings are less formal and motions made there do not need to be seconded. (There are also some special motions, such as motions of privilege, that do not require a seconder, but these are rarely included in minutes unless your organization requires a verbatim recording. For more information about the intricacies of motions, you can refer to one of the books on parliamentary procedure listed in Appendix 2.)

It is standard practice for each motion to begin with the word "that" followed by a noun and a verb, and that each motion be stated in a positive fashion. See Sample #8 for examples of the various ways motions could appear in minutes.

The minutes should state who made the motion and whether it was carried, defeated, or tabled (i.e., the vote was postponed). The reason for recording defeated motions is that the issue involved can be raised again under special conditions only.

Very formal minutes also include the name of the seconder and the names of those present and the side they voted on. Or, if the vote is by secret ballot, the minutes contain the number of votes for each side. Fortunately, few organizations require this much detail.

If you are deciding how much detail to include, you may want to refer to one of the guides on parliamentary procedure listed in Appendix 2. In *Procedures for Meetings and Organizations*, Kerr and King advise including the name of the seconder, but *Robert's Rules of Order* states that this is not necessary as it only clutters minutes with useless detail. Naming the seconder does not provide any useful information to those reading the minutes because a person who seconds a motion does not indicate acceptance of it, only a willingness to hear it discussed.

Geoffrey Standford's Third Revised Edition of *Bourinot's Rules of Order* states that it is not necessary to specify any names in the minutes unless they are directly relevant to the issue under consideration.

Because there are different acceptable standards, I recommend that you consult the parliamentary authority specified in your organization's bylaws.

## 2. Numbering systems

You may want to adopt a simple numbering system for motions so you can easily refer to them at any time. For example, Motion Number 92-45 could refer to the forty-fifth motion voted on in 1992.

Other numbering systems provide more information, such as the type of meeting, the year, the number of meetings, and the number of the motion. For example, "E:92:7:3" means the third motion at the seventh meeting in 1992 of the executive committee.

## 3. Resolutions

A resolution is a written motion, phrased in a special style with "whereas" followed by resolving clauses (what the group plans to do about it). You must include in the minutes a full description of any resolutions that were adopted, and a simple statement of any that were rejected.

As resolutions are often lengthy, you should encourage people to write out the resolution before it is given to you to record in the minutes. An example of a resolution appears in Sample #9.

When typing a resolution, follow these guidelines:

(a) Indent all lines 15 spaces.

(b) Type both the "WHEREAS" and "BE IT RESOLVED" in capital letters.

(c) Single space between the lines and double space between sections.

(d) Use capital letters and bold type if a person's name is included.

(e) Any reference to money should be written out, followed by the numerals in parentheses (e.g., two hundred dollars ($200)).

1.  MOTION: It was MOVED, SECONDED, AND CARRIED
    "That the board support the production of an educational brochure on drug and alcohol addiction."

2.  MOTION: It was MOVED by Jennifer Becevello and SECONDED that the unit hire three additional salespeople. MOTION DEFEATED

3.  Dr. Jeff Chin made a motion that Dr. Timothy Luke be granted staff privileges. Dr. Peter Thomas seconded the motion, which passed unanimously.

4.  Ms. Georgina Dodds proposed that the Information Services Branch donate $1,000 to the Save the Children Campaign. Motion passed by general consent.

5.  Mr. Roy Sconci moved, seconded by Ms. Eileen Hall, that the SK Management Company take over the operation of the Rosevale Nursing Home.
    Motion defeated.

6.  Motion No. 9X-34, moved by Cameron Ward, seconded by Paul Becevello.
    Moved, that the Board appoint the YMCA to be the operator of the child care facility opening at Queen and Main Streets in September 199-. This operator would also be responsible for the before-school, lunch, and after-school programs on the premises.

    Motion No. 9X-34 Carried.

7.  It was moved that we hold a picnic.
    It was moved in amendment by Ms. Nancy Beeker, seconded by Ms. Joan Smith:

    That we hold a picnic and a dance.

    The chair declared the amending motion lost. The question was then put to the main motion, it was resolved in the affirmative.

    *Explanation: Someone on the committee moved that the group hold a picnic. Ms. Nancy Beeker amended the motion to include a dance in addition to the picnic. The chair then asked the assembly to vote on Ms. Beeker's amendment. The group voted not to have both a picnic and a dance. The chair declared the amending motion (Ms. Beeker's) lost and then called for a vote on the main motion — to hold just a picnic. The assembly voted yes. They wanted a picnic.*

8. It was moved by Ms. Karen Giles that an ad hoc committee for community relations be established.

   It was moved in amendment by Mr. Adrian Chin that an ad hoc committee for community relations, composed of three Canadian citizens, be established. Amending motion and main motion carried.

   *Explanation: In this case, Karen Giles moved that an ad hoc committee for community relations be established. Adrian Chin amended the original motion to include the fact that the committee be composed of three Canadian citizens. The chair asked the assembly to vote on the amendment — the committee be composed of three Canadians — and the group voted in favor of this. The chair then had to ask the group to vote on the main motion — the establishment of the ad hoc committee. The results of the vote showed that, yes, the group agreed to the committee.*

The Cobden City Council moved the adoption of the following resolution:

WHEREAS, for a number of years **MARGARET BOUDREAU** has served as president of the local Cancer Society,

and,

WHEREAS, she has chaired this city's Literary Guild for two years;

and,

WHEREAS, she has been highly involved in the establishment and operation of our food bank, therefore

BE IT RESOLVED, that **MARGARET BOUDREAU** be named "Citizen of the Year," and

BE IT RESOLVED, that a donation of two hundred dollars ($200.00) be made in her name to the Cancer Society, and

BE IT FURTHER RESOLVED, that a banquet be held in her honor on Tuesday, the 22nd day of May, 199-.

# 4

# MINUTES FOR INFORMAL MEETINGS

Large assemblies generally find that their meetings run more efficiently if they are conducted on a formal basis according to parliamentary procedure. However, small groups, because of their size, their purpose for meeting, or the personalities and job rankings of the members, may prefer to operate more informally.

For example, managers who meet regularly to discuss the management of accounts or a small group of people meeting to design a new advertising campaign will probably accomplish more by either distilling or completely abandoning parliamentary procedure. However, minutes are still a vital component of these meetings and can be prepared in an informal fashion as described below: semiformal style or action style.

## a. SEMIFORMAL MINUTES

Semiformal minutes support meetings that operate on a modified version of parliamentary procedure. They report what occurred at the meeting for the people who were absent and for future reference, and they summarize the action taken, the action planned, the people responsible, and the deadlines.

If you use the semiformal style, write the minutes in a narrative format in complete sentences. Include some background information, keeping in mind that you are writing solely for the benefit of people already familiar with the group and its activities.

You can ignore the subhead groupings of the formal style of minutes, but you should begin with a heading similar to that of formal minutes, or set it up as a memo (e.g., To:, From:, and Subject:). Sample #10 shows the semiformal style of minutes.

**SAMPLE #10**
**MINUTES — SEMIFORMAL STYLE**

---

ABC Consultants' Report Meeting
November 23, 199-

The weekly report meeting for ABC Consultants was held on Monday, November 2, at 9:00 a.m. in the 2nd floor boardroom. Dr. Roy Brown presided. The consultants present included Barbara Bowen, Ryan Biss, Michele Baty, Jason Ho, and Wendy Zuliani (recorder). Penny Strachan was unable to attend.

The minutes of the previous meeting, held on October 24, were read and approved.

Dr. Roy Brown collected the written reports from the consultants on their past week's visits to ABC's nursing homes.

Dr. Roy Brown reminded each consultant to submit expense claims by the end of the day to ensure that the checks would be available at the next meeting.

Ms. Michele Baty recommended that as ABC intends to take on the management of three more nursing homes this year thought should be given to the hiring of an additional consultant.

Dr. Roy Brown said that he would discuss this with ABC management before the next meeting.

---

Mr. Jason Ho felt that a new furnace should be purchased for the Chatelaine Nursing Home as the existing one is old and may not last the winter. Dr. Roy Brown asked him to talk with the maintenance manager at the home and with the furnace company to investigate the size of a new furnace and the installation time required, and to submit a cost estimate for the November 24 meeting.

The consultants voted to reject a proposal that all ABC nursing homes adopt the same weekly food menus.

Ms. Wendy Zuliani reported on the cleaning products used in many of the homes. She found that the XYZ Company's products are as effective as any others, the costs are comparable, and the solutions come in bio-degradable containers. The consultants voted in favor of insisting that all homes use only XYZ products.

The next meeting of the consultants will be held on Monday, November 27 at 9:00 a.m.

The meeting was adjourned at 9:30 a.m.

| | |
|---|---|
| *Wendy Zuliani* | *Roy Brown* |
| Ms. Wendy Zuliani | Roy Brown, M.D. |
| Recorder | Chairperson |

## b. ACTION MINUTES

Action minutes are best suited to meetings that operate in a purely conversational manner. Like the semiformal style, action minutes are written for the people who were absent and for future reference.

Action minutes can be written in point form. You need to identify the person or persons responsible for future action and set time limits. These dates make action minutes a handy follow-up tool. As deadlines approach, a single copy of the minutes, with the deadline for future action circled or highlighted, is an excellent way to remind someone of their responsibilities.

In many informal meetings, the minute taker is encouraged to participate in discussions, or the chair may decide to assume the role of minute taker also. Some people find it difficult to take notes when they are also trying to participate in the group's discussion. One of the ways to solve this problem is to prepare your paper as follows. Draw a line vertically down the middle. On the left side of the page, record the comments of the participants. On the right, jot down your own thoughts and any questions that you might want to ask the speaker. Then, when it is your turn to talk, simply glance down at your notes.

Some groups share the minute taker's duties among the members with a different person appointed minute taker at each meeting. In these cases, you may find that the action minutes are the easiest to use; they allow you to make notes as well as participate in discussions. In addition, the straightforward format keeps the minutes consistent despite the different people involved.

Action minutes can be set up a variety of ways (see Samples #11 and #12).

**Committee:** Consultants    **Date:** November 23, 199-
**Location:** Boardroom
**Participants:** Dr. Roy Brown (Chair), Barbara Bowen, Ryan Biss, Michele Baty, Jason Ho, and Wendy Zuliani (Recorder)  Absent: Penny Strachan

**Agenda Topic:** Management of Additional Nursing Homes
**Discussion:** ABC may take on the management of three more nursing homes.

Consultants are working overtime now trying to visit company's present homes and keep up with paperwork.

Mr. Jason Ho is taking a three-month leave of absence starting January.

When will management of new homes be assumed? Where will they be located?

**Results:** The management of the new homes could be handled if an additional consultant were hired and trained before the new homes came on board.

Preferably, the new consultant should live close to one, if not all, the homes.

**Expected Action and Deadlines:** Dr. Roy Brown should make management aware of the need to hire an additional consultant if they proceed with the new homes.

Dr. Roy Brown will report on the discussion at the next meeting.

Secretary:_____Phone:_____Ext.:_____

## MINUTES — ACTION STYLE B

**MINUTES FOR:** Consultants
**Date:** November 23, 199-       **Location:** Boardroom
**In Attendance:** Dr. Roy Brown, Barbara Bowen, Ryan Biss, Michele Baty,  Jason Ho, and Wendy Zuliani

| ACTIVITY | RESPONSIBLE | DEADLINE |
|---|---|---|
| ABC is taking on the management of 3 more nursing homes. Consultants already overworked. Jason Ho taking a leave of absence. Speak to management re hiring and training a new consultant before management of new homes begins. | Dr. Roy Brown | Dec. 16 |
| New furnace is needed for Chatelaine Nursing Home — investigate size of new furnace required | Jason Ho | Dec. 16 |
| Discussed possibility of having identical food menus in all homes. Idea rejected. | | |
| All homes should switch to XYZ cleaning products — they are just as effective and cheaper than others. | All consultants | immediately |

Next meeting: December 6, 9:00 a.m. Boardroom

# 5

## TECHNIQUES FOR PREPARING MINUTES

Although formal and informal meetings are conducted differently and their minutes appear in diverse formats, your job as minute taker is the same — to prepare an accurate summation of the decisions and actions taken at a meeting.

To be a good minute taker you should —

(a) understand company jargon,

(b) have a background knowledge of the topics being discussed,

(c) know the meeting participants, or at least the spelling and pronunciation of their names,

(d) be familiar with past minutes, and

(e) have good communication skills.

This chapter offers suggestions for making the recording process a little easier and for handling additional duties that may be part of your role. As minute taker you may have duties before, during, and after the meeting.

Depending on your organization or group, not all the information in this chapter will apply to you. The recording secretary who is an official member of the organization is seldom asked to carry out the "housekeeping" chores assigned to someone who is also the office secretary. And the minute taker who records comments at an informal meeting does not usually have to worry about advance preparation.

However, as a professional minute taker, read the following information and use the suggestions that apply.

## a. BEFORE THE MEETING

If it is your first time taking the minutes for an organization, find out what is expected of you.

(a) Are you taking notes for someone else to transcribe or will you do it yourself?

(b) Are there previous minutes to examine?

(c) When are you expected to have the first draft prepared?

(d) What is the purpose of the meeting?

(e) Are you permitted to voice your own comments in the meeting or is your function simply to take notes?

(f) Will you be expected to have certain information on hand?

(g) What is the parliamentary authority used by the organization? How familiar should you be with it?

(h) Has an agenda been sent out to all the participants?

(i) Are you supposed to phone the participants and remind them of the meeting?

(j) Are you responsible for booking the room and room setup?

### 1. Booking the room

If you are responsible for booking the room, reserve it every time the date of the meeting is announced — even if your group meets there regularly — to avoid a possible meeting conflict.

If you are booking a new room, be sure it meets the needs of your committee. Is the room the right size? Will audiovisual equipment be available? Does the room have electrical outlets? See chapter 11 for more information on booking the room.

## 2. Meeting participants

In the minutes, you should always include a list of those who attended the meeting and of those who were invited but did not attend. To save time in the meeting, prepare an attendance list in advance and then check off names as the participants appear. Names not checked off will later appear in the "absent" column of the minutes. On some occasions, a quorum may be important for voting purposes so you may be expected to keep track of the time if members arrive late or leave early. This system will also enable you to quickly tell the chair when everyone is present.

If you are unfamiliar with the meeting attendees, pass a sheet of paper around the room just as the meeting begins and have the members record their names; use this list to prepare a seating plan.

To make the note-taking process easier, assign each member a number (see Sample #13), and use the number in your rough notes instead of the name. Substitute the full name when you prepare the draft minutes.

## 3. Working with the chair

As the minute taker, you should keep track of activities or decisions that were deferred to upcoming meetings and alert the chair as he or she is preparing the agenda (see chapter 10). You should also remind the chair of any correspondence to be read at the meeting or of any presentations that will be made that day.

If the assembly is to have visitors, find out all you can about the group and relay the information to the chair.

## 4. Notebook

Spiral-bound note pads are not practical for today's meetings because they don't allow enough room to record comments, especially those made out of sequence. Note pads require too

# SAMPLE #13
## SEATING PLAN AND NUMBERING SYSTEM TO FACILITATE NOTE TAKING

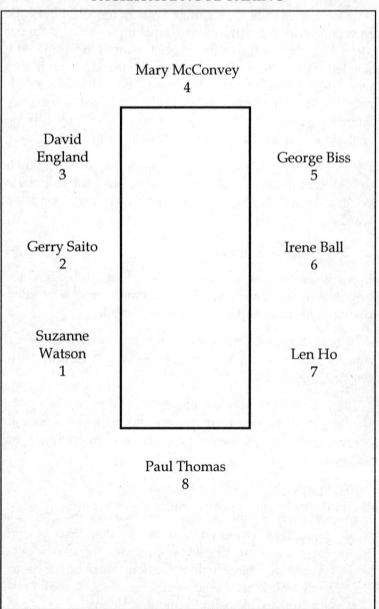

Mary McConvey
4

David
England
3

George Biss
5

Gerry Saito
2

Irene Ball
6

Suzanne
Watson
1

Len Ho
7

Paul Thomas
8

much page flipping, both during and after the meeting. A simple solution is to use a three-ring binder.

Use the agenda to organize your notebook. First, title each page with the name of an agenda topic — one page per topic. Draw a line down the page, as shown in Sample #14. The left-hand side of the page is to summarize what is said when the topic is officially discussed. The right-hand side is reserved for comments, which may be made out of sequence later in the meeting. (If the meeting is conducted by a strong chair, you will have few comments on the right-hand side.)

Another way to organize your notes during a meeting is to highlight motions and future actions with colored markers. This makes it easier to summarize the information afterward.

### 5. Previous minutes

If you are recording for a group for the first time, read the previous minutes so you will understand the type of information that the group expects you to include.

Some organizations include much rationalization and discussion, while other organizations want only the bare essentials recorded.

If you feel the minutes of previous meetings are poor, don't try to alter their format overnight. Talk to the chair in private. Some group participants are not always ready for change.

### 6. Jargon

Some groups or committees have their own vocabulary; what may be standard terminology to the members may be confusing jargon to you. Check the previous minutes for the wording. You may have to do some homework on the meaning of some technical or legal words. If necessary, make a list of terms with correct spellings and definitions.

## SAMPLE #14
## RECORDER'S NOTEBOOK

| | |
|---|---|
| **Meeting:** | **Date:** |
| **Agenda Topic:** | |

| **Discussion:** | |
|---|---|
| | |

## 7. Rules of order

How closely does your committee follow parliamentary procedure? Are you, as the recorder, supposed to know something about the rules of order?

These are important questions to find the answers to before a meeting. You should know which parliamentary authority the organization relies on as stated in its bylaws. If a disagreement does arise, that authority can be referred to.

For easy reference to the rules of order and procedure, it is always wise to have a simplified rules book with you in the event that something has to be checked. You may want to refer to *Chairing a Meeting With Confidence*, another title in the Self-Counsel Series.

Remember, too, that if an item was voted on in the past, it cannot be discussed and voted on again unless a motion is made to rescind the earlier motion. It is the recorder's job to remind the chair of the earlier decision.

## 8. Carry-in material

You will appear highly efficient if you bring the following items into a meeting:

(a) Extra copies of the agenda and material sent out with the agendas for the people who forget their copies

(b) List of attendees

(c) Copies of the group's constitution and bylaws

(d) A guide to the rules of order

(e) Minute book for the past year

(f) A list of the members of committees associated with the assembly

(g) Relevant correspondence and reports

(h) Calendar

(i) Extra pens and colored pens

(j) Binder (notebook)

(k) Watch

(l) Computer disks, if necessary

(m) Tape recorder and tapes (see chapter 9.)

## b. AT THE MEETING

If room setup is part of your job, it is important that you arrive early to ensure that everything has been prepared according to your instructions.

Are you responsible for providing note pads, pencils, glasses, and water jugs? What about the audiovisual equipment?

Arriving early also helps you to stay calm and relaxed — an important frame of mind for a recorder.

### 1. Seating

A recording secretary or minute taker who is also an officer of the organization should sit on the left-hand side of the chair. (The position to the immediate right of the chair is reserved for special guests.) An office secretary or outside recorder may be seated at a small, separate table near the chair. Obviously, the table should be placed so that the minute taker can see all the speakers during the meeting.

Some minute takers like to sit at the opposite end of the table from the chair, but this is the worst location for two reasons. First, the recorder's job is to be an advisor to the chair in terms of information contained in previous minutes, and this can't be done from a distance. Second, a good chair insists that all comments be directed through him or her. Therefore, members normally spend much of their speaking time facing the chair and speaking in a voice loud enough to be heard by the chair. If the recorder is sitting beside or near the chair, hearing a member's comments should not be a problem. Besides, the seat at the end of the table is an ideal spot for someone who is going to make a lengthy presentation.

## 2. Reading the minutes

If the minutes have been distributed, they are not read aloud. But at general meetings, which the entire membership is invited to attend, a "reading of the minutes" is a fairly common practice. The reading is done by the minute taker. To avoid any embarrassment, have the minutes unofficially approved by the executive group beforehand. Neither you nor the group want to look foolish by having mistakes read aloud. As well, practice reading aloud before the meeting to avoid too many "ers," "ums," or incorrect emphasis.

## 3. Corrections

The first thing a chair does when he or she opens a meeting is to ask the participants to approve the minutes of the last meeting. At this point, the meeting participants may either approve or ask for changes or corrections in the minutes.

According to *Robert's Rules of Order*, an assembly may correct the minutes at any future date by a simple vote, no matter how much time has elapsed or how often they have already been amended. Obviously, only the people who were present at that meeting may participate in the vote.

Any necessary changes or corrections are made either in the affected minutes or in the minutes of the meeting when the change was requested if a vote is required. If everyone agrees to the alteration, the recorder makes the change on the affected minutes by drawing a line through the incorrect portion and inserting the new material in longhand. In the margin next to the correction, write the date of the meeting when the minutes were corrected and have the chair initial it.

If the correction is lengthy, then the change is retyped on a separate piece of paper. Draw a line through the edited version and note in the margin on what page a correction appears. On any such correction page, include a signature line for the minute taker and another for the chair. Be sure to also include the date.

If the group disagrees about the change, then the change must be made by amendment, which will appear in the new minutes. Make a handwritten note in the previous minutes about the amendment.

If members frequently request changes to your minutes, try to resolve the problem immediately after the meeting by reviewing your summary notes with the people concerned. If necessary, you may have to start using a tape recorder to verify what was discussed.

### 4. Computer systems

Nowadays, some minute takers use a lap-top computer to record the minutes directly at a meeting. They claim that it saves them time since all the information is keyed directly into the machine. Someone who is a good touch typist can type and keep his or her eyes on the speaker — a good listening technique.

This system can also be used for quick referral to previous minutes if the minute taker has the disks from earlier meetings readily available.

### 5. What to record

Whether you are using shorthand, longhand, or a computer, remember that only the motions and resolutions are taken down verbatim. (It is a wise idea to ask the members to put all complicated motions in writing.) The rest of the minutes are an objective summation of what actually occurred.

Pay close attention to the discussion. You will find it helpful if you know why a topic is being discussed. Is the group's purpose simply to obtain information, or is its aim to eventually reach a decision? If this is the case, your notes should be progressive. If the purpose is to solve a controversial problem, you should have a number of pros and cons recorded. Never inject your own personal bias or give one person's comments more weight than another's.

Here are some guidelines.

(a) Record:

- All pros and cons
- New information
- All motions (passed and defeated)
- Results of motions
- Expected action

(b) Do not record:

- Speaker's experiences
- Old material
- Redundant information
- Withdrawn motions (**Note:** some authorities may suggest to record these)
- Personal comments

Try to analyze why the person is speaking and how the comments relate to the topic under discussion. Concentrate on the relevance of the speaker's words rather than on the delivery or the word choice.

At one public hearing on a zoning variance, the speaker so mesmerized the board with a description of how the noise from his neighbor's house caused him to have an extramarital affair and his wife to leave him that the chair forgot to call a halt to the "soap opera" histrionics. Fortunately, the recorder quickly realized that none of the material could be included in the minutes so she put down her pen and enjoyed the show.

Your references to each topic may be as brief or elaborate as the organization wishes. Yet, each item of business must be included even if it is just one sentence.

The chair's role is to ensure that all members have an opportunity to talk on all issues, so you may hear the same points repeated frequently. However, record a comment only once. If a point has already been made, don't record it again.

Your group should decide whether it is necessary to include a name with every comment. Try to avoid this. If the chair does not keep strict control and the members speak out whenever they wish, it is difficult to list who said what.

If you must feature names, be consistent in the way you refer to people. Do not call one person "Ms. Bowen" and the other "Bill Jones," for example. It may be unintentional, but a lack of consistency in titles or names may indicate a preference for one person over another. One recorder gripes that she has to remember to feature the comments of a different member for each meeting; otherwise, the participants end up with hurt feelings. Not only is this a nuisance, but sitting on the edge of your chair waiting for a specific individual to say something noteworthy creates a lot of unnecessary stress.

Never use the minutes personally to commend or criticize something that is said or done at the meeting. Avoid any personal comments, judgments, adjectives, or adverbs that suggest good and bad qualities. For example, never write "Mr. Smith's capable assistant read an excellent report on delivering programs to special education students." The minutes should not be your interpretation of what happened, only your organized version of what was said.

In writing up the results, state whether a decision was made, action taken, or the issue left unresolved or deferred to another meeting. The bylaws of some formal assemblies require that the names of all those voting on each side be recorded, or if the vote is by secret ballot, the number of votes on each side. Fortunately, most organizations do not require this amount of detail.

Relax and avoid panicking if you miss a point. Chances are that if it is a major one it will be restated later or you can contact a speaker after a meeting to confirm the wording. At the same time, avoid doing this frequently or you will appear unprofessional. Don't hesitate to ask the chair to call a temporary halt if you are falling behind.

On occasion, a chair or member may state that the following discussion is confidential or held "in camera." This means that there is no formal record of the discussion. In this event, make it obvious to everyone that you are not taking notes — put down your pen. Do not use the time to update or clarify earlier statements because meeting participants may think you are recording their comments even though you were instructed not to do so.

If using a recording device, remember that it should only be used as a back-up. Chapter 9 offers helpful suggestions for using a tape recorder.

## c. AFTER THE MEETING

If you don't have time to prepare the minutes immediately after a meeting, at least reread your notes to ensure that they are sufficiently detailed so you can interpret them later.

According to memory studies performed at the University of Minnesota, immediately after you listen to someone else talk you can recall only 50% of what was heard. This percentage drops even lower after one week — down to 10%. As the minute taker, you cannot afford to depend on your memory to recall important decisions.

### 1. Rough draft

Your drafts should be labelled "Rough Draft" and double spaced to allow for corrections and editing. Be sure that the idea you want to express is clear in your mind before you begin to write.

(a) In formal and semi-formal minutes, always write in complete sentences using the past tense and the third person. Never use abbreviations; type a person's name in full. In action minutes, point form is acceptable.

(b) In formal minutes, words such as "Committee," "Board," "Department," or "Division" are capitalized, as well as titles: "Secretary," "President." In informal minutes, these words are not capitalized unless they are accompanied by a specific name. For example, in "the committee wishes…" use a lowercase "c". However, in "the Education Committee wishes…" use capitals.

(c) Use a straightforward, narrative style and simple words. If the group is concerned only that the minutes be intelligible to them, you can be brief in your comments. If the minutes are a means of communicating with others, then your summaries should be in essay style.

(d) Headings or subheadings should not be left dangling at the bottom of a page; they should be followed by at least two lines of text or moved to the next page.

(e) Circulate the rough draft to as few people as possible or it will take forever to get the minutes written (everyone will have his or her own version of what occurred).

(f) Use subheadings for individual topics in the body of the minutes. Each item on the agenda can become a separate heading.

(g) Double check all figures, dates, and spelling of names.

Always keep your notes of the meeting until the minutes have been formally approved by the group.

## 2. Final draft

As minutes are normally filed in binders, use the bound manuscript format — 1.5 inches (4 cm) on the left margin and 1 inch (2.5 cm) for the right, top, and bottom.

The heading lines should begin 1 inch (2.5 cm) from the top of the paper and each heading line should be centered. The words can be typed in either upper- and lowercase letters or in capitals depending on the organization's official style.

If the minutes are brief, double space the body and triple space between items. If they are long, single space them with a double space between paragraphs. Indent paragraphs ten spaces unless you are using subheads. If you are, it is not necessary to indent. Place the subhead directly above each paragraph.

Use **bold face** for subheads and to highlight dates and names (if you are working on a computer which has boldface capability).

## d. THE MINUTE BOOK

### 1. Filing the minutes

Official copies of the approved or amended minutes are kept by the recorder in chronological order in a binder set up for that particular year. The cover page of the minute book may read:

*The Minutes of the Literary Society*
*of Teesdale County*
*from January 1, 199- to December 31, 199-*

The minute taker normally has custody of the minutes and all the other official documents that come before the assembly. Every member, however, has the right to inspect the minutes, and the chair can order that certain minutes be turned over to a committee that needs them to perform its duties. People who wish to see the minutes but are not on the committee should be referred to the chair for permission.

The minute taker is also responsible for storing committee reports and documents submitted at meetings. Before filing this material, note on the covers the dates they were received and state any further action that was taken.

## 2. Indexing the minutes

Indexing your minutes will take a few more minutes of work, but it will go a long way toward building your professional image. Remember, as minute taker, you are also the group historian and, therefore, are responsible for identifying what happened in previous discussions. An index will allow you to quickly produce any relevant minutes.

An index is an alphabetical listing of all the main items discussed at meetings. Along with the topic, list the date it was discussed and the page number where the information can be found in the minutes. Each time the topic comes up again, place the new date and page number below the previous reference.

Some minute takers prepare their indexes by using a 3" x 5" card (see Sample #15). Others prefer to use a computer listing. One highly professional minute taker uses the card system and pulls out the appropriate cards when she is making up the agenda. If a topic is not already listed, she makes up a new card at that time. She also carries the cards with her into the meeting in case she is required to update the group on past activities. When her minutes have been approved, she adds the page numbers to her file cards and returns them to the index.

If you have no experience indexing, current indexing computer programs might be helpful. These programs help you identify key words and then automatically alphabetize your headings and identify them by page number.

Whether you are using cards or a computerized system, the information on each topic should include the subject, date of the minutes, and the book and page where the topic can be found. Each time a topic is raised at a meeting, add the new date and place beneath the previous reference on the file card.

Library collection

April 17, 199-, Book 1, page 45.

September 15, 199-, Book 3, page 34.

### 3. Motions book

Some groups that do not make many motions may prefer to use a motions book rather than an index. The motions book contains all the motions and amendments ever made by that particular assembly with the dates that they were made. If you place blank sheets of paper between all the typed pages, you will have space to record any amendments to a motion directly beside the original material.

### e. BYLAWS AND PROCEDURES BOOK

The minute taker should also have all the rules that the assembly uses to govern itself — the constitution, bylaws, rules of order, and standing rules — combined in one book or binder that may be carried into all meetings.

Insert blank pages between all the written material so you can add any amendments directly on the page opposite the original article. Remember to include references to the dates and pages of the minutes where discussion of the actions can be found.

## f. KEEPING INFORMATION CONFIDENTIAL

In some meetings, you may be responsible for recording highly confidential information. Never leave your notes lying on your desk even if they are in a folder. Keep them in a locked drawer until you are ready to work on them. If someone comes to talk to you, carefully cover your typewriter or clear your computer screen.

Resist the urge to tell someone "just a little." Take a firm stand if you are pumped for information. Suggest that the person inquiring contact the chair if he or she really wants to know.

In addition, remember to protect your diskettes if you are using a personal computer. Label all diskettes with the date and other relevant information and store them in a safe place.

If you have confidential information on your computer, do not assume that you have erased it by pushing the "delete" key. You would be surprised how much a computer hack can retrieve. If it is essential that you get rid of certain information, you must initialize the disk.

# 6

# PARLIAMENTARY PROCEDURE: THE DEMOCRATIC PROCESS

## a. WHAT IS PARLIAMENTARY PROCEDURE?

Generally, groups of ten people or more find that they can achieve their objectives more efficiently if their meetings are run according to parliamentary procedure. Parliamentary procedure is a general name given to a predetermined series of rules that has been developed over the centuries. The rules, which apply equally to all participants, help an organization carry out the following activities:

- Elect leaders

- Bring forth ideas

- Debate those ideas

- Refine them

- Reach decisions

The rules also prevent meetings from turning into shouting matches or from being taken over by unqualified people.

There are a number of reference guides on parliamentary rules available to organizations. Some of the more common authorities are *Riddick's Rules of Procedure, Mason's Manual of Legislative Procedures, Bourinot's Rules of Order*, and *Demeter's Manual of Parliamentary Law and Procedure*. A more recent book, designed specifically to meet the needs of the general public, is *Procedures for Meetings and Organizations* by M. Kaye Kerr and Hubert W. King.

Yet, the most widely used reference guide in North America today is still *Robert's Rules of Order*. It was originally written by the American general, Henry Robert, in 1876, and it has been updated over the years.

Once an organization has chosen its parliamentary authority, the choice should be stated in the bylaws. (See Appendix 2 for a list of books on parliamentary procedure.)

In this book, the information provided regarding parliamentary procedure is based on *Robert's Rules*.

## b. UNDERSTANDING THE RULES

It is important that both you and the chair be familiar with the basic rules of your organization's chosen parliamentary authority. The variations may be slight, but they are important to the governing of the meeting and the recording of the minutes. For example, *Robert's Rules* declares that it is not necessary to record withdrawn motions, while Kerr and King state that withdrawn motions must always be listed in the minutes.

A professional minute taker will always take a copy of the organization's parliamentary reference book as well as the organization's constitution and/or bylaws into the meeting in the event of a dispute or query.

As recorder, you should remember that the ideal chair is one who can remain impartial at a meeting. The chair should have no friends or enemies at the time of the meeting and should give everyone equal hearing. To maintain an air of formality in the meeting, the chair should insist on addressing everyone by Mr., Mrs., Miss, or Ms. and the last name. The chair should also be referred to as the Chair, Madam Chairman, Mr. Chairman, or whatever formal address that he or she chooses.

The chair is the traffic cop of the meeting, handling disputes and directing the flow. A good chair normally insists that all the speakers' comments be directed through him or her. However, if a participant feels that a speaker is not following correct procedure or that the comments are irrelevant, the participant can call a "point of order." If the participant wishes to question the speaker or the chair, he or she calls a "point of information."

Incidentally, in a large, formal meeting, a gavel helps a presiding officer to maintain control. It is seldom used, except for a light tap to indicate that the meeting should come to order or to signal adjournment, but it remains a visible signal that a formal meeting is underway. It also serves as a subtle reminder of where the presiding authority rests.

According to *Robert's*, the chair may vote when the voting is done by ballot and if his or her vote will make a difference. For example, if the vote is nine to ten in favor of a motion, the chair may vote against the motion making the vote ten to ten. The motion is automatically lost because of the tie. (A main motion can only be carried if there is a majority vote.) However, the chair is never forced to vote — even to break a tie.

*Bourinot's Rules of Order* states that in a large, formal meeting the chair has no vote, but he or she may cast a vote in the event of a tie. However, in less formal meetings, the chair may participate in discussions and vote on any issue.

Some organizations operate differently and want the chair to be part of all proceedings. These groups may abide by *Robert's*, *Bourinot's*, or some other form of parliamentary procedure, but in their bylaws, they give the chair two votes. The first vote is equivalent to a member's regular vote and the second is used to break ties.

Appendix 1 at the back of the book has a simplified list of the terms with which a professional minute taker should be familiar when taking minutes at a formal meeting.

## c. MOTIONS

A motion is a formal proposal placed before the meeting by one of its members. Another member must second the motion (agree to the motion being discussed) before any debate may begin. If the motion is not seconded, the motion dies and does not need to be recorded in the minutes.

If a motion is made and seconded, the chair (or the recorder at the request of the chair) should restate the motion to the group to ensure that everyone understands what is being discussed. This is a perfect time for you to ensure that you have copied down the motion accurately.

It is a good idea for the chair to insist that all proposers of motions — especially complicated motions — put their motions in writing and give them to the chair, who later turns them over to you, the minute taker.

The mover of the motion is generally extended the right to open the discussion and to close it before the vote is called.

All other members may then speak on the issue. According to *Robert's*, after everyone has had a chance to speak once, members may speak a second time. Then the person who made the motion has the opportunity to sum up. However, some organizations limit members to one opportunity to speak. They may also include a time limit.

The chair's job is to act as a referee and to ensure that everyone has equal opportunity to comment. Whenever possible, the chair should alternate the people speaking for and against a motion. The chair can only add his or her personal comments by temporarily relinquishing the chair to someone else. (This is a privilege that should be used infrequently and only if the chair feels strongly about an issue.)

A motion can be amended, and an amendment may even be made to an amendment. But amendments to the third degree are not permitted.

Only one main motion can be considered at a time. However, there are three other classes of motions that take precedence over the main motion on the floor: subsidiary, incidental, and privileged motions.

### 1. Subsidiary motions

Subsidiary motions affect the main motion. They are the motions to —

(a) postpone indefinitely,

(b) amend,

(c) commit or refer,

(d) postpone definitely,

(e) limit or extend debate,

(f) close debate (call the previous question), and

(g) table the motion.

Although most motions require a majority vote to pass, the motions to limit or close debate require a two-thirds vote because they infringe on the rights of the members. Another difference in subsidiary motions is that while the first four listed above are debatable, the last three are not.

### 2. Incidental motions

Incidental motions arise out of other motions and, therefore, take precedence over and must be decided before main or subsidiary motions. However, they yield to privileged questions and cannot be amended. The five incidental motions are —

(a) suspend the rules,

(b) appeal the decision of the chair,

(c) objection to consideration of the question,

(d) reading papers, and

(e) withdrawal of a motion.

Incidental motions, except for the motion to appeal, cannot be amended.

### 3. Privileged motions

Privileged motions are not related to the main motion but are important to the safety, orderliness, or comfort of the members. They take precedence over all other motions and cannot be debated.

The four privileged motions are —

(a) call for the orders of the day,

(b) questions of privilege,

(c) to adjourn or recess, and

(d) to fix the time of the next meeting.

## d. PRECEDENCE OF MOTIONS

It is possible to have so many motions before an assembly that the group won't know which to consider first, so all motions have been assigned a ranking or precedence, according to their function. The following is a brief outline of the precedence of motions with the highest ranking motions appearing first:

(a) Fix the time of next meeting

(b) Adjourn

(c) Recess

(d) Questions of privilege

(e) Call for the orders of the day

(f) Appeal

(g) Lay on the table

(h) Close debate

(i) Limit or extend debate

(j) Postpone definitely

(k)  Commit or Refer

(l)  Amend

(m) Postpone indefinitely

(n)  Main motion

Any time one of these motions is being discussed, any motion higher on the list can be considered; any motion lower on the list is out of order.

For example, if a main motion is made and someone moves to postpone it until the next meeting, that motion is valid because it has a higher ranking than the main motion. Before the vote on the postponement, someone could move to recess, but no one could move to amend the motion because a motion to amend is lower than the motion to postpone to a given day.

Motions are voted on in the reverse order to which they are presented. The last motion proposed is voted on first, then the next motion and back to the main motion.

# 7

# INTERACTION: A NEW MEETING STYLE

The traditional style of meeting discussed so far is not particularly suited to informal problem solving, collaboration, or for working out complex, interdependent issues. Nowadays, progressive organizations are cutting meeting time with "interaction" meetings.

Reva Nelson, President of Words•Worth Professional Communications in Toronto, teaches this new approach to meeting management to North American businesses in "Meeting for Results" seminars. According to Ms. Nelson, interaction meetings are more productive, energetic, and democratic. In conventional meetings, the chair normally has the most authority. The chair controls how the meeting proceeds, talks more than anyone else, and is responsible for the final decisions. This can affect group participation and morale and can result in poor decision making.

## a. THE ROLE OF THE FACILITATOR

In the interaction-style meeting, the chair separates procedural and decision-making responsibilities and appoints someone to handle a new role — facilitator. This enables the chair to sit and listen fully to the opinions of the group.

The facilitator's job is to accomplish a specific task. The facilitator must solicit opinions from the entire group, ensure that everyone feels comfortable with the process, and keep the meeting on target.

The facilitator is assisted by the recorder, who ensures that all the members' main points are written on large sheets of paper taped to the wall in front of the group. In this way, everyone has a clear and immediate understanding of what is being said and can see that all statements are accurate. As all ideas are considered to come collectively from the group — not from individuals — the names of the originators of suggestions are not recorded.

Both the facilitator and recorder must remain neutral and refrain from voicing their opinions or editorializing. If either one feels the need to make a personal statement, he or she must ask the group's permission to temporarily step out of the assigned role.

An ideal situation would have all the members of the group taking turns to act as facilitator and recorder. In fact, the facilitator and recorder may even be invited from an outside department or group.

Seating arrangements are another difference of the interaction meeting. The conference table is removed and the participants are seated in a semicircle facing the wall. Large sheets of paper are taped to the wall, and the recorder lists the title of the topic being discussed and the page number at the top of each sheet.

Ms. Nelson, who bases her work on the theories of Interaction Associates in the United States, says that while the traditional style of meeting can be compared to a traditional family gathering with the chair as the father, the secretary as the mother, and the participants as the children, the interaction meeting can be compared to a joint bus trip.

"The facilitator acts as the steering wheel and guides the bus. He controls the speed and the direction. The group members are the passengers. Everyone has to agree on the destination and take responsibility for ensuring a good trip. After all, the steering wheel can't move the bus, and the wheels can't control it. The desired outcome and the agenda receive the most attention before the bus even begins to move."

## b. MEMBERS MORE ABLE TO PARTICIPATE

Interaction meetings are highly creative and productive. Members feel less intimidated and have equal opportunity to participate in brainstorming and problem-solving sessions. They leave feeling heard, validated, and energized. They have specific tasks to accomplish.

For example, one company in Vancouver had considered switching to flex time but had vetoed it after arguments presented at the company's regular monthly meeting and the chief executive officer's unequivocal "no way." The topic was later raised at an interaction meeting and, since all the participants were encouraged to present their opinions for and against without fear of being shouted down, new and valid points were introduced. The new information was then presented to the company's management as a more representative picture of how the employees actually felt, with solutions to possible problems that could occur.

## c. TAKING MINUTES AT AN INTERACTION MEETING

Obviously, this chapter is a simplification of how the interaction meeting works; there are many more details to consider such as the meeting summation, agenda preparation, time frame, and number of participants. However, if you are appointed recorder at an interaction meeting, remember that your role is always to support the facilitator and the group.

As a recorder, you must have —

(a) good listening skills,

(b) legible hand writing,

(c) an understanding of the group's jargon,

(d) confidence to ask the group to slow down if you fall behind in the recording, and

(e) a nonjudgmental expression.

It is important that you, as recorder, not put words in the mouth of a slow-thinking participant. Be quiet. Talk as little as possible. Defer your questions to the facilitator. You are his or her teammate and support person.

When listing the group's comments, make the letters about 1 inch to 1½ inches high (2.5 cm to 4 cm). Don't worry about your spelling. You can use abbreviations, circle key words, or use arrows and signs. Use colored markers to highlight ideas. Remember to number and title all pages. Get the members to restate any points you have missed or misrepresented. The meeting members share the responsibility for accurate recording.

After the meeting, remove the pages from the wall, label, and store them or have them typed. The recorder is also responsible for preparing a summary sheet or action minutes. See chapter 4 for ideas on writing action minutes.

# 8

## ELECTRONIC MEETINGS

Electronic meetings use electronic tools to convey information or to share ideas. Experts predict that as companies expand their operations and technology improves up to 40% of future meetings will be electronic.

There are three ways to meet electronically:

(a) Video conferencing

(b) Teleconferencing

(c) Computer conferencing

## a.  VIDEO CONFERENCING

Video conferencing uses satellite transmissions to link two or more groups of people meeting in specially equipped rooms. Participants can both see and hear their counterparts. Many large hotel chains now offer this type of electronic meeting to their clients.

Video conferencing can have one- or two-way video. One-way transmissions are essentially private TV transmissions to a select audience. This type of transmission is used for activities such as announcing new policies to a company's national sales force.

Although it is expensive to do, a company may set up and operate its own permanent video conferencing sites. This can save time and money in the long run because executives are not tied up traveling across the country repeating the same presentation to different audiences.

Two-way video conferencing means that all the participants can see and hear one another. It involves smaller and more elaborate facilities. Each location normally consists of a soundproof room containing a conference table and one or more wide screen monitors. Cameras provide coverage of the participants, charts, or other visual material.

## 1. Advantages

Video conferencing is a useful tool if you want to —

- reach an audience of at least 200 people scattered across the country or the world,

- present technical or detailed information,

- use photographs, product demonstrations, or other visual aids, or

- motivate or train your audience.

## 2. Disadvantages

For video conferencing to be practical, staff must be able to meet in groups of at least 25 people. Besides the cost, video conferencing requires extensive lead time and coordination. Broadcast and receiving sites must be carefully investigated. You also have to be careful to coordinate your presentation to be convenient in all time zones.

Most video conferences are held in locations specifically designed for that purpose; they do not normally take place within the regular work setting, which means that each participant must spend time traveling to the meeting.

Another disadvantage to video conferencing is that participants may feel self-conscious about appearing on camera, which can affect the spontaneity of the meeting and the natural flow of ideas.

In addition, discussion can be difficult at a video conference because members are less under the control of a chair than they would be in face-to-face meetings. Participants also complain that it is difficult to interpret "talk-turn" signals so members tend to interrupt at inappropriate moments. This makes it difficult for the minute taker to attribute comments to specific individuals.

### 3. Instructions to the minute taker

- If a presenter is making a prepared speech, try to get a copy that you can condense for the minutes.

- If you appear on the video screen, wear a solid-color, dark suit or simple dress. Play down jewelry — some pins, rings, earrings, and hair ornaments can cause reflections, which are usually seen as irregular blotches in the TV picture. Also avoid colors that contrast too brightly such as a white shirt and navy suit. Blue is a good color for a shirt.

- It can get hot under the lights so don't dress warmly.

## b. TELECONFERENCING

Teleconferencing, or conference calling as some people call it, is ideal for situations requiring a speedy exchange of information. Teleconferencing usually involves two or more groups of people conversing via telephones.

As the locations are usually widely spread, the savings in travel time and money are substantial. (The cost of teleconferencing is based on telephone time, so the meeting should start on time.) During the meeting, participants may use fax machines to transmit documents.

Conference calls can be made directly by the chair or through a telephone operator. If the chair wishes to handle the call, the chair can either —

(a) call participants and connect them as needed, or

(b) have all participants dial in to a specifically reserved number at a prearranged time.

The alternative is to have a telephone operator call and connect all the meeting members.

There are, however, several problems related to teleconferencing:

- Some people have trouble interacting with others they can't see.

- Confusion can result when people talk at the same time or out of turn.

- The pace can be slow since people tend to speak more slowly and distinctly on the phone.

But these problems can be minimized, if the chair carries out the following suggestions:

(a) Prepare an agenda and circulate it before the meeting so that everyone will be prepared and have necessary material handy.

(b) Begin the meeting with an introduction or roll call of all the participants. If several people are meeting at the same location, insist that they choose just one person to voice their comments.

(c) Follow with a short orientation message on the purpose of the call.

(d) Insist that all members identify themselves before they speak: Bob here, I …

(e) Direct all questions to specific people: John, how do you feel about …?

While the teleconference is underway, the chair is the only person who should speak without being called upon. The chair should also make sure that the meeting starts on time and he or she should end the teleconference by summarizing the discussion and thanking each of the participants.

If minutes are required, use a telephone jack to tape the meeting as a back-up. Be sure that all the members know they are being taped.

Remember that an agenda is the key to teleconferencing. It is prepared in the same manner as a standard agenda; however, since the participants can't look around the room and see who is in attendance, be sure to list the participants' names and positions. You should also include in the heading the special conference call number that the members must use if they are dialing into the meeting.

Companies who teleconference regularly circulate profiles and photos of each meeting participant once a year. New profiles are sent out as new members are added. This helps reduce the problem of the "faceless" voice.

In addition, it helps to send out all visual materials before the meeting. Make sure that the materials are easy to follow and numbered to match the agenda items.

## c. COMPUTER CONFERENCING

Large computer network systems allow individuals to communicate across large distances within the same time frame or on a delayed basis. This means that the information can be entered at the sender's convenience; receivers can obtain the information at the time of transmission or at their convenience. "Meetings" can be short or they can continue over an extended period.

Computer conferencing has the same drawback as teleconferencing: no visual cues to make communication easier. In addition, as the words are not vocalized, it is impossible to pick up information from voice inflections and tones.

On the other hand, there is no specific group limit and as everything is already typed and filed, you don't have to worry about "faulty memories."

# 9

## USING A TAPE RECORDER

It is impossible for a minute taker to take verbatim notes at a meeting unless he or she can take shorthand at approximately 250 words per minute. Fortunately, few meetings require this type of transcription. Most need only a summary of what occurred.

However, a tape recorder can be a useful back-up tool for checking the exact wording of motions or precedent-setting decisions or to clarify points mentioned in your notes.

In addition, the chair of an informal meeting may decide to use a tape recorder rather than appoint a minute taker. Instead of taking notes, the chair can quickly repeat major points into the machine during the meeting. Later, the comments can be typed and distributed. As minute taker, you may also want to use a tape recorder as proof of the accuracy of your notes if the chair or participants frequently correct the minutes.

### a. PREPARATION

The tape recorder can be a mixed blessing. Like everything with mechanical parts, it can act up when you least expect it. If you are caught with a faulty recorder, you will be blamed — not the machine. Remember Rosemary Woods of Watergate fame and her infamous machine, which erased "important" information!

Here are some guidelines for operating recording equipment.

## 1. Before the meeting

(a) If you have not used a particular model before, read the instruction manual and practice.

(b) Re-test your equipment the day before the meeting.

(c) Check how much recording time you have on each side of the tape cassette. Although cassettes are the same size, they do have different recording capacities. Take along more than enough tapes.

(d) If the device is battery operated, check the strength of the battery and have spare batteries on hand.

(e) Pick up an extension cord if you need one to plug the machine into the wall; check the outlet the day of the meeting to ensure that it is working.

## 2. At the meeting

(a) Let the participants know at the beginning of the meeting that you are using a recording device.

(b) During the meeting, check the machine periodically to see that the reel is turning, the voice-recorder is in a desirable position, and the tape has not run out.

(c) A good machine has a tape counter. Periodically include the counter figures in your notes. Later if you want to check a comment, you know approximately where it can be found on the tape.

## 3. After the meeting

(a) Label the tape with the group name, meeting time, date, and location.

(b) Develop a policy for keeping the tapes: how long should you keep them (at least until after the minutes are approved at the next meeting); where they will be stored; and who has access to them.

A word of warning: if you are making a recording for someone else to transcribe later, ensure that you use a tape cassette that will fit the playback unit of the transcriber. For example, imagine the dilemma of one young secretary who found on her desk one morning a minicassette and a note from her boss. She was to type up the notes of his meeting with a customer and send them off to the president of the company immediately. The minicassette had been prepared on the sales representative's personal machine just before he left for a week's vacation. None of the company's machines was able to handle a minicassette!

## b. PURCHASING A TAPE RECORDER

There are numerous tape recorders on the market today that can easily help you record a meeting. They can range any-where from $40 to $2,000.

The ideal recording machine for meetings has the following features:

(a) An easy-to-read counter so that you can retrieve specific information later

(b) A means of signalling the end of a tape, a broken tape, or no tape

(c) An A/C adaptor

(d) A voice-activated mechanism, which automatically starts and stops the machine when someone begins or stops speaking

(e) A mute control to filter out background noise

(f) A telephone jack if you are involved with teleconferencing

(g) A microphone jack for large meetings

Sony, Panasonic, GE, Metzer, and Lanier all make good machines. I have talked to several people who spend large portions of their week working on minutes. They recommend Dictaphone's ExecTalk Plus. It has all the above features plus a digital clock, and can also be used for dictation.

Dictaphone's Dictamite II is a portable recorder which can be purchased in either a micro or mini format. While it doesn't have all the benefits of the larger machine, it is great for both dictation and minute taking and is small enough to be carried in a briefcase. (Both Dictaphone models are those available at the time of printing.)

# 10
## THE AGENDA

## a. THE IMPORTANCE OF THE AGENDA

Preparing an agenda is not part of the minute-taking process, but many recording secretaries help the chair to write and circulate one. The purpose of an agenda is to familiarize all the participants with the topics that will be discussed at the meeting, ensure that they all have the same expectations regarding the outcome, and that they come prepared to make their contributions.

A chair should never schedule a meeting and then design an agenda. Instead, he or she should decide what must be achieved and then prepare an agenda that will help the group reach these goals. The chair can provide valuable information by including on the agenda an estimate of the time required to handle each item. This also gives the chair more control during the meeting.

## b. CHOOSING THE AGENDA TOPICS

Some chairs prefer to involve the members in the preparation of the agenda so that everyone has a voice in the meeting organization. A chair can do this by the following methods:

(a) Phoning the members before the agenda is prepared

(b) Distributing a tentative agenda and asking for comments

(c) Waiting until the meeting and asking for approval or amendment of the proposed agenda

(d) A combination of all three methods

In addition, because you are the minute taker, you have a unique familiarity with the meeting's activities, and you should remind the chair of any special decisions or actions that have been deferred to this particular meeting. These items should be included in the agenda.

## c. THE LAYOUT OF THE AGENDA

### 1. Style

The heading on the agenda should be consistent with the heading on the minutes; it should include the full name of the organization and the particulars of the location and time. If the meetings move from city to city, include the name of the city. The word "agenda" can go at the top or bottom. The letters can be in upper- and lowercase letters or in capitals, depending on the organization's style (see Sample #16).

For groups that meet frequently, a "grocery list" agenda is acceptable because certain items will have been regularly discussed and familiar to each member. However, a good agenda provides more than a list of topics to be covered. A proper agenda includes descriptive words and phrases that let the participants know what will happen at the meeting and what is expected of them (see Sample #17).

These words could include —

- review,
- analyze,
- update,
- determine,
- decide, and
- finalize.

The chair should also include the estimated time required to discuss each subject and the names of anyone who has been asked to have a special report ready on the topic.

AGENDA
BOARD MEETING
COBDEN PUBLIC LIBRARY SYSTEM
7:00 PM, TUESDAY, MAY 9, 199-
BALMORAL ROOM
CENTRAL LIBRARY


or


Board Meeting
Cobden Public Library System
7:00 p.m., Tuesday, May 9, 199-
Balmoral Room
Central Library


Agenda

AGENDA

STAFF MEETING

MICROPAK ENGINEERING LTD.

9:00 A.M., TUESDAY, MAY 9, 199-

BOARD ROOM

630 KING STREET

Discussion of parking problems at the Finlay Plant:
Lloyd Cummings                              10 minutes

Announcement of new health regulations:
Safety Committee                            5 minutes

Update on the installation of air conditioning at
Ajax office:
Jack Davis                                  10 minutes

Decision on the vendor for the new computer system:
                                            15 minutes

Meeting to adjourn at 9:45 a.m.

If any of the members are coming from out of town, you may want to enclose a map with directions to the site as well as recommendations for transportation and accommodation.

### 2. Teleconference agenda

The headings for an agenda announcing a teleconference vary slightly. Add the dial-in number if the members must call a specific number to join the meeting. Also include a reference to the time zone being used if the participants work across the country.

Include the names of the chair and the other people who will be participating (see Sample #18). This will help the participants to prepare questions or to gather information in advance.

### 3. Numbering system

Some organizations prefer to use a numbering system for both the minutes and the agenda to make it easy to refer to specific items of business. One popular code refers to the type of meeting, the year, number of meetings, and the item of business. (To identify the type of meeting, a letter is used: A = annual general meeting, G = general meeting, B = board, E = executive committee, NC = nominating committee.) Therefore, the code "B:92:3:6" indicates the sixth item of business at the third board meeting of 1992. This system can also be adapted for numbering motions.

### 4. Informal meeting agenda

If the meeting is run on an informal basis, the chair has a lot of latitude when it comes to choosing the order in which the various topics will be discussed.

Here are some guidelines for the best positioning of topics:

(a) List the most important item first so that it gets adequate coverage.

## TELECONFERENCE AGENDA

Date of Teleconference: April 25, 199-

Time of Teleconference: 11:00 a.m. E.S.T.

Dial-in Number: 1-416-555-7856

Subject: Mining Exploration Program in Wilhelm Township

Chairperson:
Marcia Ruthes, Vice-President - Toronto

Participants:
Bruce Watkins, Treasurer - Toronto

Glen George, Senior Geologist - Kenora

Janice Polley, Geologist - Pickle Lake

Sam Smith, Land Acquisitions - Winnipeg

Agenda

1. Status of Drill Holes
    1.1. B - 80 Drill Hole
    1.2. B - 83 Drill Hole
2. Reports on Land Acquisitions in Wilhelm Township
3. Reports on Financial Statements

(b) List topics relating to only a few of the members last so those participants not involved with the particular topics can leave early.

(c) Group similar items together.

(d) Put controversial items near the end as members are less likely to disagree; sandwich them between two positive items.

(e) Always try to end the meeting on a positive note.

(f) Include the expected time of adjournment.

### 5. Formal meeting agenda

The proceedings of a formal meeting are standardized so laying out the agenda is a relatively simple process following the same organizational pattern as a formal meeting, as shown in Sample #19.

## d. CIRCULATING THE AGENDA

Although an agenda can be presented to the members at the meeting, the standard practice is to send it out beforehand to allow the participants time to reflect on the topics and, if necessary, to do research and gather information.

Agendas should be sent out at least three days before a meeting. A week is preferable. If you must send an agenda by mail, allow extra time.

If a particular topic requires the reading of background material, send the information out with the agenda, but remember to take extra copies to the meeting for the people who forget to bring theirs.

Once the agenda is sent out, you can organize your notebook according to the agenda topics (see chapter 4).

On occasion, a person may be asked to make a presentation at a meeting that he or she does not ordinarily attend. Instead of sending out an agenda, you need only send a brief letter or memo informing the presenter of the date, time, and

## Agenda
Board Meeting
Trident Public Library System
8:00 p.m., Thursday, May 26, 199-
Main Floor Meeting Room
345 Queen Street

**Approval or Correction of Previous Minutes**

**Reports**

Comparison of two proposed computer systems:
Jack Davis                                    20 minutes

**Old Business**
Decision on the hiring of an administrative assistant
                                              10 minutes

**New Business**
Discussion on a proposal for an internal newsletter:
Marlene Russell                               15 minutes

**Announcements**
New payroll procedure                         5 minutes
Christmas Party                               5 minutes

**Adjournment**                               9:00 p.m.

location of the meeting, and the time at which he or she is expected to speak. This kind of notice is shown in Sample #20.

## SAMPLE #20
## NOTICE TO GUEST PRESENTER

### MEMO

To: Ms. Cynthia Speaker

From: Ms. Rita Remindher


There will be a meeting of the Environmental Advisory Council at 10:00 a.m., Thursday, March 3, 199-, in the Board Room on the 3rd floor, 783 Bay Street, Toronto. The Chair, Mr. George Jones, asks that you be present and be prepared to give your presentation from 11:15 a.m. to 11:45 a.m.

# 11

## BEHIND THE SCENES

Many minute takers are also involved with the arrangements behind the scenes. In other words, they are responsible for selecting and booking a room, overseeing the room setup, and arranging for refreshments.

If these are your responsibilities, the following information should make your life easier and help you appear highly efficient.

## a. BOOKING THE ROOM

Naturally, the first thing you must know when organizing a meeting is the date and time of the gathering. Ideally, you should have several months' notice for a hotel booking and at least two weeks' notice to ensure an appropriate room in the organization's headquarters. The meeting location should be included in the agenda.

If the meeting is to be held in the company boardroom and there is no booking to be made, tape a neatly printed and courteous note to the door of the boardroom the day before to confirm your use of the room. You might also notify anyone sitting just outside the room that you plan to use it. Perhaps he or she can help you keep it available.

### 1. Check the facility

Book the room as soon as you know the date of the next meeting. Even if the meeting is held at the same place on a regular basis, confirm the booking each time to avoid any confusion.

If you are booking a room you have never used before, ask these questions:

(a) Is the room kept locked? Who has the key?

(b) Does the room have audiovisual equipment?

(c) Are there any windows that might affect slides or overhead projections?

(d) Is there a microphone system?

(e) How do you control air conditioning, lighting, and background music?

(f) Who do you call in an emergency?

(g) Who is responsible for setting up the chairs and tables?

If the meeting is going to be held at an off-site facility, don't take anything for granted. Confirm all the details in writing and get a commitment for a specific room so that you can't be bumped. Besides asking the above questions, find out about the quality and service of refreshments and about the other activities going on in nearby rooms that day. Will they conflict with your meeting?

I remember attending a meeting at a well-known hotel in Toronto. Halfway through the meeting, a public auction for oriental rugs began in the next room. The resulting din made it impossible for the participants to interact. At our request, the hotel moved us to another room, but it took a while for the participants to get back on track.

## 2. Choose the right size of room

The size of the room will have an effect on the meeting. For example, a small group of ten people will feel intimidated in a large auditorium. Sounds will echo and hearing may be difficult as the voices are not contained.

If the room is too small, it will quickly become hot and stuffy. Members may feel uncomfortable and even claustrophobic. They will generally not converse freely.

If you must choose between a too-large and a too-small room, think about the effect you want to create. A little crowding (not too much) may encourage a team spirit. Also, don't forget that it is possible to make a large room appear smaller by partitioning off parts of it.

The British House of Commons was intentionally designed to hold only two-thirds of its membership. That is all that usually shows up, so the place never seems empty. For the occasional crisis, the crowding only heightens the feeling of urgency of the debate.

Gender and age can also affect room selection. An all-female group is usually comfortable in a small room, but may be more competitive in a large one. A group of males in the same small room will be competitive, but will be more comfortable in a large room. In addition, the older the participants, the more space they prefer around them.

## b. SEATING ARRANGEMENTS

The meeting's purpose should be a major consideration when deciding on the seating. Psychologist Harry Levinson, a Harvard University industrial consultant, says "A human being is a source of energy and most of it radiates in the direction he or she is facing."

According to the "sources of energy" school of thought, meetings conducted around a round or oval table do not tend to be as productive as those grouped in other seating arrangements. This is because the sources of energy are directed inward toward the people sitting opposite; this critically restricts and cancels the energy flow.

Therefore, if the meeting's purpose is to solve a problem, don't seat the participants at a round table. However, if you want a friendly, brainstorming session to develop, the round table works well unless the participants are naturally hostile to one another. If this is the case, the round table will only intensify the anger and aggression.

If the participants are meeting to hear a formal presentation or a report, they will work best at a rectangular table with the chair at the end of the table farthest from the entrance to the room. This arrangement is suitable for groups with less than 20 people. For a larger group, a classroom style approach is best.

To encourage groups of approximately 30 people to interact and enter into discussions, use a U-table formation.

Behavioral scientists recommend a semicircle arrangement facing the leader for problem-solving meetings. Ideally, the semicircle is placed away from the door so that the people coming and going will not disrupt the meeting.

## c. SETTING THE ATMOSPHERE

The physical setting of the meeting has a significant psychological effect on the participants. Formal settings are appropriate for making important announcements, signing contracts, or introducing new senior staff. However, formal settings are not conducive to solving problems.

If you want participants to become totally involved, you need an informal space where people can push their chairs together, hang papers on walls, and interact in comfort.

Ventilation, good lighting, and comfortable chairs are also important. Remember it is better to start a meeting with the room on the cool side.

In addition, the atmosphere of the meeting is influenced greatly by the behavior of the participants. If the people are comfortable with each other and with what is expected of them, they will participate more freely and be more productive in meetings. The chair should take some time at the beginning of meetings to let the group warm up and to be sure that everyone is introduced.

## d. REFRESHMENTS

If the meeting is going to run over several hours, it is a good idea to have some sort of refreshments available. For a morning meeting, arrange for coffee, tea, juice, and possibly some rolls or muffins. Soft drinks go well in the afternoon. Cheese or fruit trays and containers of yogurt add a special touch.

According to a study by psychologists Robin Kanarek and David Swinney of Tufts University in Medford, Massachusetts, a mid-afternoon snack helps invigorate the mind. Apparently, a candy bar, a cup of yogurt, or a diet soda consumed around 3:30 p.m. increases the memory and alertness of most individuals by approximately 15% to 20% despite what was eaten for breakfast or lunch. Possibly the increase in blood sugar from the snack gives the brain a jolt that lasts an hour or two.

A friend of mine once worked for a very authoritarian boss who called an 8:00 a.m. meeting. He had one pot of coffee brought in and told his staff that the meeting would continue until all their problems had been fully resolved. There were to be no breaks for additional coffee or lunch. By 2:30 p.m., eight very hungry and angry people left the room. Several decisions, which had been made simply to hurry the meeting along, had to be reworked in later meetings. Incidentally, shortly after that the boss was moved to another position within the company — one that did not require people management skills.

# 12

# HOW HIDDEN VARIABLES AFFECT
# MINUTE TAKING

There are several obvious factors that can influence a meeting: the chair, the agenda, the room setting. But there are also hidden variables that can affect the group's interaction, as well as what is recorded in the minutes.

These hidden variables include group size, status of participants, body language, seating, reasons for membership, personality types, and communication styles.

While it is not necessary for a minute taker to fully understand group dynamics or body language, some background in these areas can —

- make the meeting more interesting;

- prepare you for what to expect during the meeting in terms of member participation, the speed of decision making, problem solving, and conflict resolution;

- make it easier to obtain an accurate message; and

- assist in determining what should be included in the minutes.

If you'd like to find out more about meetings and how people interact socially, see Appendix 2 for a list of recommended titles.

## a. GROUP SIZE

Group size has a direct influence on the behavior of each individual within a group. For example, as the size of a group increases, the average member's participation declines. In other words, in a large group you will find that only a few people will freely voice their comments. This may be because members feel intimidated by the size of the group or because comments similar to theirs have already been voiced by the more talkative members.

Meeting experts suggest that meetings should be limited to 15 people. A larger size is difficult for the chair to control and inhibits input from the whole membership.

Here are other interesting notes on group size:

(a) Groups of six tend to be highly productive, while the productivity of larger groups often decreases.

(b) Groups of six have a high team spirit, while groups of four may be troubled by internal conflicts.

(c) People working in groups of five are usually comfortable working within their groups; people in groups of seven or more are often unhappy because of communication and coordination problems created by larger groups.

(d) Small groups handle simple problem-solving tasks better than groups of five to twelve. Groups of the larger size seldom reach unanimous agreement on problem solving as the members have a wide range of opinions.

## b. STATUS OF PARTICIPANTS

Meeting participants tend to allow people of higher status to dominate a meeting and its discussions. They often overlook or pay little attention to the knowledge and expertise of a person they perceive to be of lower status.

Status within a group devoted to business interests usually comes from a person's ranking in the office hierarchy. A perfect example of this occurs in the movie *Working Girl*. Actress Melanie Griffith plays a secretary who firmly believes that her brilliant advertising idea will be heard only if she masquerades as her boss, and, as it turns out, in her particular situation she is correct.

As a professional minute taker you must be unbiased in the recording of discussions. Take care that you don't pay more attention to the comments of one person over another because of his or her position on the corporate ladder.

If you are attending a meeting of people of equal status, you may find that the discussion travels in circles; the chair has to work at keeping everyone on track. There may be a lot of complaining within the group, and you may see some power struggles occur.

If membership cuts across the normal structure of the organization, the members have to work out their new working relationships before they can become an effective group. Many comments may not relate directly to the topic on hand as members seek recognition by "strutting their stuff."

## c. BODY LANGUAGE

People normally derive their status by their position within an organization, but the body language of some people may give them authority that perhaps they don't deserve. On the other hand, others unconsciously downgrade their status within a group by their mannerisms.

People can make themselves appear more powerful in a group situation by being well dressed, walking tall, seeking eye contact, speaking confidently and clearly, and using "open" gestures. Others will listen to their opinions.

People who appear deferential, who continually nod, smile, hold their arms close to their body and their legs close together, tend to come across as people of lower status. Their comments may often be overlooked or attributed to the "higher status people."

Many women assume a deferential posture out of politeness and do not realize what it does to their stature within the group.

People who give off inaccurate status signals create problems within a meeting both for the participants and for the minute taker. Watch that a person's body language does not overly influence your decision either to discard or to include certain comments within the minutes. Listen for the real message.

## d. SEATING

Watch where people sit in a meeting. Where participants choose to sit in a meeting often indicates how they perceive their status and power within a group. Some seating positions tend to be more influential than others. People who see themselves as having a high impact on a meeting usually seat themselves at the head, foot, or in the middle seats of a rectangular table. People in these positions tend to communicate more.

After these positions, the "good seats" are the ones beside the people who are deemed to be of importance.

Spatial or seating arrangements also determine the flow of communication within a group and between the group members and the chair.

- If the chair is inclined to be passive, group members generally talk more with persons facing them across the table than with the people sitting beside them.

- If the chair is strong, members will interact more with their neighbors than with the people opposite.

- At a meeting of five people seated around a rectangular table, with three people on one side and two on the other, the two-person side will have more influence on decision making.

## e. MEMBERSHIP

To operate efficiently and to be truly productive, a group must have competent members dedicated to achieving the same objectives. Otherwise, meetings may drag on and accomplish little.

If membership of the group is based on political considerations, the group may lack expertise in some areas. If a group's members are appointed without being consulted, they may not be prepared to become seriously involved or to devote the necessary time to the group. Committees consisting of volunteers may be hampered if the participants joined for the prestige or visibility and do not have the expertise or the interest to work at the task.

In Velma Seawell Daniels' delightful book, *Celebrate Joy*, she writes about her experiences on a committee so prestigious that the membership kept growing until the only way to get anything done was to appoint subcommittees. At one point, Ms. Daniels found herself appointed chair of the "Subcommittee to Reassess and Define Atmospheric Changes in the Supplemental Learning Center." In other words, the group was supposed to clean up and redecorate the children's library at the church. Fifteen people were appointed to the subcommittee, eight actually showed up, and five did the work. That sounds about right!

## f. PERSONALITY TYPES

Certain behavior patterns or personality traits can also affect a person's contributions to a group activity.

Shy or introverted people voice their opinions quietly and infrequently. Yet, fewer contributions translate to less influence in the business meeting. Shy individuals are interrupted more and often retreat into silence if their ideas are debated.

Extroverts behave in the exact opposite manner. Since they exhibit self-confidence and are aggressive in their speech, the group is more likely to listen to their opinions. Some extroverts are impulsive talkers and need an experienced chair to keep them from monopolizing or taking control of the group.

Some people are overachievers with a high record of accomplishments. They are hard driving, competitive, impatient, and aggressive. While overachievers may do well in certain areas, meetings can bring out the worst in them as they have difficulty working as a team. They are often impatient with their fellow members, interrupt or finish the sentences of others, and try to speed up the pace of the meeting. They hate to delegate as they feel they are the only ones who can effectively carry out a task.

Authoritarian people enjoy rules and regulations. They believe in power and hierarchical decision making. When acting as a chair, they use their power to direct and control others. They can be demanding and dictatorial. However, as meeting participants, they are submissive and readily follow instructions.

The manipulator is another personality type that may show up in a group. Manipulators are those who spend their time influencing others toward their own goals rather than the group's objectives. Manipulators are shrewd and highly persuasive and they do not allow concerns like friendship, loyalty, or morality to affect them.

There is bound to be some degree of personality conflict within any group. However, the experience of the chair, the maturity of the members, and the group's determination to achieve its goals will determine whether these differences have an impact on the group's operations.

When you act as the minute taker, you must remain completely neutral and your minutes must not show any partiality or antagonism toward a particular member or members.

# g. COMMUNICATION STYLES: MEN AND WOMEN

While there is little difference between men and women in their personality types and management styles, there are some basic differences in their communicative behaviors which can affect a meeting. As a professional minute taker you must be aware of these differences.

In business meetings you will find that men will seize their turns to speak while women wait their turns. Men tend to interrupt more than women, and women usually stop speaking when they are interrupted. A woman's comments may be overlooked or ignored due to frequent interruptions or louder voices. Few men are even aware of this problem.

Traditionally, men are much more direct in their language style than women. Men will say, We must do this. While women will ask, Don't you think, we should...? Men speak positively, while women tend to end their sentences with an upward inflection — the sign of a question.

Men use fewer words and more commands: Wait! Women, on the other hand, pepper their speech with pleasantries, use more words to say the same thing, are more likely to talk about feelings, and use more intensifiers and qualifiers in their speech: Just a minute, please. I personally feel... This program is not carved in stone, but...

Questions rather than statements and hesitant versus confident speech make it difficult for the recorder to decide whether a comment should be added to the minutes. This often results in an idea being attributed to the group or to a more confident-sounding voice than to the person who originally made the comment.

Beware of the differences in language styles of men and women and try to give equal weight to the comments of both sexes.

# 13

## A FINAL WORD TO MINUTE TAKERS

### a. THE MINUTE TAKER'S IMAGE

I know many minute takers who love their jobs and enjoy working with both the chair and the members. However, I have also met people who are not happy being assigned the role of minute taker and who frequently complain about the other people involved.

When I think about these two groups of people, it seems that there is a great difference in their personalities and body language.

People who are happy in their jobs tend to be more positive both in their outlook and in their mannerisms. Minute takers who are unhappy in their role and complain that they are treated as second-class citizens, are ignored, or are criticized unfairly, tend to behave — often unconsciously — in a fashion that encourages this sort of treatment.

Granted, some people are just not suited to be minute takers, just as some people do not make good chairs or good managers. And it is possible for personality differences to create problems within working relationships. However, sometimes it is the image that the minute taker projects to the chair and to the group that may be at the root of the problem.

I have seen people at meetings whose face and posture show that they are unhappy about having to take notes. Obviously, they don't understand the importance of minutes in helping a group to function effectively. Nor do they fully comprehend the essential role that the minute taker plays within the meeting structure (see chapter 2).

However, it's not enough to know that you are of consequence in the meeting environment, you must project your belief to others. If you appear confident about yourself and your abilities, others will automatically assume you are competent and worthy of notice. Obviously, the work that you later submit will confirm or deny this first impression.

## b. CONVEYING A SUCCESSFUL IMAGE

But how do you convey a successful image?

Research shows that appearance counts for 55% of what people think about you on a first impression, and how you speak counts for 37%. What you have to say — the actual words — counts for only 8%.

In other words, even if you do not have a speaking role at a meeting, people are still going to make some judgment about you and your abilities. Now I am not saying that these assessments will be accurate or fair, but they do happen and they will be based on your appearance and your body language.

Here are some guidelines for projecting a confident image within a meeting setting.

### 1. Clothes

Clothes are important. While they don't make a person, they do make a difference. Dress like everyone else in the group, although stay on the conservative side. Never wear anything showy or aggressive because showy clothes show that you fear you won't be noticed, and confident people never worry about that.

### 2. Make contact

The chair hosts the meeting and the minute taker is the chair's assistant. So remember the parting and greeting rituals. Say hello when members arrive, or raise your eyes and smile if they are across the room. After a meeting, cheerfully say goodbye or see you tomorrow.

Always shake hands; it's the universal opening ritual of any business interaction. Make sure that your grip is firm but not overpowering. Make eye contact.

### 3. Use body language to influence people

Remember your work at a meeting is important. Don't slouch. Walk tall. When seated, don't curl over or hunch your shoulders. Some people expand their space in a meeting by filling out their chests and extending their arms and legs. Others tend to shrink within their personal space by minimizing their body size. This projects a submissive image.

If you want to encourage someone to keep on talking, lean forward, nod, and smile slightly. If you want the speaker to explain a point in more detail, raise one eyebrow or cock your head. Cupping your hand behind your ear will encourage him or her to speak up.

On the other hand, as minute taker it is also important that you learn to develop a "poker face" and not show any emotion regarding a member's comments.

Eye contact is important in business settings and to help with the listening process. However, it should not be confused with staring. In North America, a polite listener will focus on the forehead, chin, or mouth, catching the speaker's gaze occasionally. It is normal for eye-to-eye glances to last a second or less.

What we perceive often becomes reality. If you believe that the chair or a member is hard to deal with, chances are he or she will be. Your beliefs will cause you to project unconscious signals which can affect others.

For example, if you are speaking with someone you think dislikes you, you may find that your lips are pursed, your body is rigid, and you have trouble making eye contact. These signs may be subconsciously absorbed by the speaker, who will feel antagonistic toward you. You manufactured the feeling. Think positively about your interactions with others.

Too many smiles can correlate to low status and power, but too few smiles show a negative attitude. It can be hard to find the happy medium. Smile when it feels right and genuine.

If you have an opportunity to voice your own comments at a meeting, remember:

- Speak loudly and clearly.
- Look directly at the chair and then at the other members.
- Sit or stand tall.
- Know your subject thoroughly.
- Be prepared.

Learn to relax and enjoy yourself. As minute taker, you have an excellent opportunity to learn about an organization and see how decisions are made. Your task as minute taker is an important one and can be a rewarding and interesting career opportunity.

# APPENDIX 1
# PARLIAMENTARY TERMS — SIMPLIFIED

**ABSTAIN**

To deliberately refrain from voting.

**ACCLAMATION**

No one has opposed the election of a candidate.

**ADJOURN**

To halt the proceedings until another time and/or to another place.

**AMEND**

To change an item by adding, removing or inserting a word or words.

**BYLAWS**

Regulations that govern an organization. They may be found in the constitution or described in a separate document.

**CENSURE**

An official reprimand.

**CONSTITUTION**

A statement of an organization's basic objectives, structure, and methods of operation.

**EX OFFICIO MEMBER**

Usually the presiding officer who appointed the committee. This person cannot vote but must receive all relevant reports, agendas, and minutes.

## FISCAL YEAR

The financial year of an organization.

## FLOOR

A motion to be considered has the floor. A person formally recognized by the chair to speak has the floor.

## GENERAL CONSENT

Unanimous agreement (no one objected).

## IMMEDIATELY PENDING

The business now before the meeting.

## INCIDENTAL MOTIONS

Motions that arise out of other motions.

## MAIN MOTION

A formal proposal placed before a meeting to be debated and a decision reached.

## MAJORITY

More than half the total voting group present at a meeting. In some cases, when the rights of the group will be affected by the decision, a two-thirds majority is required.

## MOTION TO AMEND

A motion to change an item by adding, removing, or inserting a word or words.

## MOTION TO COMMIT

This motion is made when an issue seems to require additional investigation or when the discussion would be too time-consuming for the general group. A motion to commit may refer the issue to an already established group, or it may set up a special group to handle the matter.

## MOTION TO REFER

Another term for a motion to commit.

## MOTION TO POSTPONE DEFINITELY

This motion postpones action on a particular subject to a definite time in the future.

## MOTION TO POSTPONE INDEFINITELY

If this motion is successful, it effectively kills the original motion for the rest of the session.

## OBJECTION TO THE CONSIDERATION OF A QUESTION

A method to prevent discussion of an issue. Must be made before any debate begins.

## ORDERS OF THE DAY

The items to be discussed as that day's business.

## PLURALITY

The largest number of votes cast but less than a majority.

## POINT OF INFORMATION

An expression used by a participant to indicate that he or she wishes to ask a question of the speaker or the chair.

## POINT OF ORDER

An expression used by a participant if he or she feels that the speaker is not following correct procedures or that the speaker's comments are irrelevant.

## POINT OF PARLIAMENTARY INQUIRY

An expression used by a participant when he or she seeks an immediate answer to a question regarding the procedure being used at the meeting.

## PRIVILEGED MOTIONS
Motions that affect the safety, orderliness, or comfort of the members or that affect the honor of an individual member.

## PRO TEM
For the time being.

## PROXY
A signed paper that authorizes a person to cast the signer's vote. An instructed proxy tells the signer how to vote, while an uninstructed proxy has no limitations.

## PUTTING THE QUESTION
Calling for a vote.

## QUORUM
The number of people — usually the majority of the organization's members — required to hold an official meeting. The number constituting a quorum is found in an organization's constitution or bylaws.

## READING PAPERS
An incidental motion to read papers before voting.

## RECESS
A brief interruption in a session.

## RECONSIDER
To review and vote on an issue that was previously disposed of.

## REFER
To direct an issue for consideration to a committee for further study before a decision is made by the main body.

## RESCIND
To cancel a previous action.

## RESOLUTION

A motion written in a formal style.

## SUBSIDIARY MOTIONS

Motions that are made to do something to the main motion.

## SUSPEND THE RULES

To change the order of the adopted agenda. Requires a two-thirds vote.

## TABLE

A motion to place a main motion and all amendments to it in the secretary's book without further discussion. A motion is later required to take the motion "from the table."

# APPENDIX 2
# RECOMMENDED READING

## a. MEETINGS AND GROUP DYNAMICS

Berezowsky, Joyce. *Organizing Business Meetings.* Edmonton: Falken Publishing, 1983.

Burleson, Clyde. *Effective Meetings.* New York: John Wiley & Sons, Inc., 1990.

Doyle, Michael and David Strauss. *The New Interaction Method: How to Make Meetings Work.* Chicago: Playboy Press, 1976.

Dunckel, Jacqueline. *Business Etiquette.* Vancouver: Self-Counsel Press, 1992.

Dunckel, Jacqueline and Elizabeth Parnham. *The Business Guide to Effective Speaking.* Vancouver: Self-Counsel Press, 1984.

Fletcher, Winston. *Meetings, Meetings.* New York: William Morrow and Company, Inc., 1984.

McMahon, Tom. *Big Meetings, Big Results.* Agincourt, Ont.: Gage Educational Publishing, 1988.

Morton, Anne. *The Office Management Manual.* Vancouver: Self-Counsel Press, 1991

Mosvick, Roger K. and Robert B. Nelson. *We've Got to Start Meeting Like This.* Glenview, Ill.: Scott, Foresman and Company, 1987

Parr, Jim. *Any Other Business? How to be a Good Committee Person.* Toronto: Clarke, Irwin & Company Limited, 1977.

*The Professional Secretary's Handbook.* Boston: Houghton Mifflin Company, 1984.

## b. PARLIAMENTARY PROCEDURES

Bliss, Ed. *Please Come to Order.* Guilford, Conn.: Audio-Forum, 1981.

De Vries, Mary A. *The New Robert's Rules of Order.* New York: New American Library, 1989.

Jones, O. Garfield. *Parliamentary Procedures at a Glance.* New York: E.P. Dutton, 1971.

Gordon, F.L. *Parliamentary Procedures Simplified.* Toronto: Coles Publishing Company Limited, 1978.

Kerr, M. Kaye and Hubert W. King. *Procedures for Meetings and Organizations.* Agincourt, Ont.: The Carswell Co. Ltd., 1988.

Stanford, Geoffrey. *Bourinot's Rules of Order.* Toronto: McClelland and Stewart Limited, 1977.

Paul, Kevin. *Chairing a Meeting with Confidence.* Vancouver: Self-Counsel Press, 1992.

# INDEX

## OTHER TITLES IN THE
## SELF-COUNSEL SERIES

**CHAIRING A MEETING WITH CONFIDENCE**
*An easy guide to rules and procedure*
Kevin Paul, B.A., M.A.

Do you need help running a meeting? The basic purpose of a meeting is to conduct your business in a fair, orderly, and expeditious manner. The rules of order used to run formal meetings can be confusing and intimidating. Why, then, do we use them? Because they work! This is not a rule book but a simple guide on how to run a meeting according to those rules. It is intended for people who have little or no experience running or participating in meetings. It is written clearly and concisely without unnecessary jargon or obscure references. $7.95

**THE BUSINESS GUIDE TO EFFECTIVE SPEAKING**
*Making presentations, using audio-visuals, and dealing with the media*
Jacqueline Dunckel and Elizabeth Parnham

Give dynamic speeches, presentations, and media interviews.

Effective communication has always been the key to business success, and this book provides a straightforward approach to developing techniques to improve your on-the-job speaking skills. This book is as easy to pick up and use as a quick reference for a specific problem as it is to read from cover to cover. Whether you want to know how to deal with the media, when to use visual aids in a presentation, or how to prepare for chairing a meeting, this book will answer your questions and help you regain your confidence. $7.95

# ORDERING INFORMATION

All prices are subject to change without notice. Books are available in book, department, and stationery stores. If you cannot buy the book through a store, please use this order form. (Please print)

## IN CANADA
Please send your order to the nearest location:
Self-Counsel Press, 1481 Charlotte Road
North Vancouver, B. C. V7J 1H1
Self-Counsel Press, 8-2283 Argentia Road
Mississauga, Ontario  L5N 5Z2

## IN THE U.S.A.
Please send your order to:
Self-Counsel Press Inc., 1704 N. State Street
Bellingham, WA  98225

Name_____

Address_____

_____

Charge to:
❑Visa          ❑ MasterCard

Account Number_____

Validation Date _____.

Expiry Date_____

Signature_____

❑Check here for a free catalogue which outlines all of our publications.

In Canada, please add $2.68 for postage and handling ($2.50 postage and $.18 GST).  Please add GST to your book order.

In U.S.A., please add $2.50 for postage and handling.  WA residents please add 7.8% sales tax

YES, please send me:

_____copies of **Chairing a Meeting With Confidence**, $7.95
_____copies of **The Small Business Guide to Effective
            Speaking**, $7.95